"We became a hot
item in the press."
*Photo credit:
Harry Langdon*

"Priscilla possessed
something more
than beauty."

"I yearned to put down roots, to share my dreams with someone."
Photo credit: Frank Lieberman

"Our love of Elvis brought us together..."

"A STAR-STUDDED KISS AND TELL."
—*Hollywood* magazine

"The title and nature of the kiss-and-tell book promises oodles of scandalous gossip.... Edwards does not disappoint...cool, understated, controlled, with no rancor toward Priscilla."
—Knight-Ridder Newspapers

"FASCINATING."
—*Sacramento Union*

"...but his ghost drove us apart."

"GRAND PASSION...JUICY, TRUE-ROMANCE STYLE."
—*Publishers Weekly*

"Tear-jerking...many famous names...and even guest appearances by the late King."
—*Seattle Times*

"HOT STUFF, A SPELLBINDER!"
—*Chattanooga Times*

"A SHOCKER!"
—Oakland *Tribune*

PRISCILLA, ELVIS AND ME

PRISCILLA, ELVIS, AND ME

MICHAEL EDWARDS

ST. MARTIN'S PRESS/NEW YORK

PRISCILLA, ELVIS, AND ME

Copyright © 1988 by Michael Edwards.

Postscript to the Paperback Edition copyright © 1989 by Michael Edwards.

Library of Congress Catalog Card Number: 88-18846

ISBN: 0-312-91643-4   Can. ISBN: 0-312-91644-2

Printed in the United States of America

St. Martin's Press hardcover edition published 1988
First St. Martin's Press mass market edition/September 1989

10 9 8 7 6 5 4

To Charlotte Edwards, my mother and inspiration

Acknowledgments

Ellis Amburn, for being by my side every step of the way

Al Lowman, for preparing me for my search within and showing me how to peel back the layers

Nancy Coffey, for her constant energy, enormous spirit, numerous powerful creative contributions, and opening up my feminine self. And for relentlessly insisting on "MORE," always making me go deeper

Tom McCormack, for demanding reason and clarity and giving his personal insight and valuable input

I appreciate all the help I've gotten from St. Martin's Press

PRISCILLA, ELVIS AND ME

Prologue

Priscilla Presley came into my life when I was at the top of the world, at the pinnacle of my career, in love with life and all the possibilities it had to offer. As the most successful male model in the United States and Europe for almost ten years, leading a dazzling existence of beautiful women, fast cars, fine wines and yachts, I yearned to put down roots, to share my dreams with someone. I found that someone when I met Priscilla.

For a time we were a golden couple, sharing our mornings locked away from the world, making love and having breakfast in bed. But this was all history now. With Priscilla Presley's success in *Dallas*, she had found a new fascination—herself. And it was taking over her life. She was consumed with her career and status as one of the world's most beautiful women. The main focus of her life now was dealing with agents, scripts, contracts, publishers and, lately, the expanding Graceland Enterprises, which she administered as the ex-wife of Elvis Presley and mother of his sole heir, Lisa Marie.

As we sat at the kitchen table in our Beverly Hills home, Priscilla picked gingerly at her breakfast, eager to depart for New York to appear in "Night of a Hundred Stars" at Radio City Music Hall. She rarely accepted invitations to celebrity benefits, and it made me suspicious—why was she looking forward to this particular one?

As she folded and unfolded her linen napkin, I didn't have to ask if there was something other than the flight that was making her tense. In a long-lasting relationship such as ours, lovers reach a place where they begin to think as one, and any sudden change of behavior by one partner is immediately noticed by the other.

I remembered another time, before leaving on a publicity tour, when Priscilla had looked as uncomfortable as she did this morning. I'd thought it was her fear of flying, but when I'd picked her up at Los Angeles International on her return from her trip, she'd looked worried and asked me if we could go somewhere for a talk before returning to the house.

"I have to tell you something," she'd said.

She'd refused to talk about it in the car, so I'd driven us to a little park in Playa del Rey, which was near the ocean. We'd walked along the beach, neither of us speaking for a while. Then she'd begun to cry and confessed to me that, after her tour, she'd flown down to Miami to Julio Iglesias.

"We didn't do anything, I swear," she'd told me. "I just couldn't get you out of my mind. On the flight home I felt as if I'd die before I got back to you. Please forgive me, Michael. It's you I love."

Now, as we sat together before she left on another trip, I couldn't help remembering that time with Julio, and I assumed that in New York she was again planning some romantic rendezvous.

"I'm sick of what we've become, Priscilla. I tried to tell you when you first got into this business, it would change you."

"Please don't start," she said. "My manager will be here any minute, and I don't want him to see us arguing again."

"I don't want us to argue. I want to talk. But all you seem interested in anymore is your workaholic manager."

"Maybe it's because he doesn't yell at me all the time."

"Your manager this, your manager that—I've had it up to here with him."

"Why are you so angry with him?"

"Because you spend more time with him than you do with me. And maybe you've forgotten—I'm your man."

"It's business. I have to."

"Do you have to call him a big teddy bear?"

"Damn you, Michael! You've been going through my diary."

She was right.

The couple who worked for us came in, carrying a basket of fresh cut roses from the garden. Feeling the tension between us, they refilled our coffee and left us alone.

For years Priscilla and I had been very secretive about our fighting, and no one, not even her parents, realized that we were frequently in trouble. We'd been so discreet that the press and rag mags regularly pictured us as the perfect Hollywood couple. Priscilla and Elvis had been the same, concealing their marital conflicts from the public and keeping their private life a mystery for years, until certain members of his staff exposed them in the book *Elvis—What Happened?*

I looked outside at the blaze of color in the flower garden

and wistfully thought of all the lazy afternoons I'd enjoyed digging and planting there. I'd tell Priscilla, "Dig your hands in. Get a good handful of earth. Feel it. It's what we're all about." But I never could get her interested in gardening. She was too concerned about ruining her nails. We'd laugh and she'd bring me tea and we'd talk while I gardened. I really loved this place, filled with seven years of memories, seven years of being a family.

"What about Lisa?" I asked. "What's she doing this weekend, while you're off in New York?"

"She'll be at my mother's."

"Lisa hates being stuck there all the time."

"That's really none of your business. While she lives in this house, she'll do as I say."

"It's my house, too."

"No, it's not."

I slammed my full coffee cup down on the table. The cup shattered, splashing coffee on Priscilla's silk robe. Leaping up, she glared at me, saying, "You've ruined my new robe."

She started to run from the kitchen, but I went after her, grabbing her wrist.

"Let go of me!"

"No. That robe means more to you than *we* do."

She struggled, but I pinned her against the refrigerator door. She fought back angrily, trying to free herself from my grip. I forced her down onto the floor on her back, straddling her.

"That's the last time you lose your temper with me," she screamed. "Get off me! I hate you!"

"Who've you got your sights set on in New York?"

"No one, damn you! Let me off the floor!"

"Excuse me. I wouldn't want to tarnish your image. I'll leave that to Julio or Richard Gere."

"That's it, Michael. We're finished!"

"We're not finished until I say so."

"I don't want it any more. Get out of here!"

"I'll get out when I'm ready, and by God I won't be coming back this time."

I'd completely lost control, but anger and frustration were running me now. Looking down at her face, I saw hatred in her eyes, and at that moment, I didn't like myself any more than she did. What man can feel good about himself after he's mistreated the woman he loves? I climbed off her and let her get up off the floor.

In that kitchen, I was torn by my lingering love for Priscilla, a violent jealousy, and the humiliation of losing her to another man.

Instinct is the voice of the soul, that first, immediate thought before you start censoring everything. When you go against it, you've gone against the urge of your spirit. My instinct had told me years ago to escape, walk out the door, throw off the suffocating cape of the Presley legacy. I had ignored that prompting. I'd tenaciously held onto my position as Elvis's successor, letting myself be mesmerized and sucked into the Elvis aura until nothing of the real me was left. I'd grabbed for the golden ring and, in the process, lost myself. All my life I had fought for control, wanting to be my own man. Elvis made me realize I could dream, and I became enormously successful following that dream to being my own man. But I'd lost all joy and satisfaction in what I had been. Destiny had somehow thrust all this on me, but I didn't want it anymore. I just wanted some uncomplicated time to find again the person I'd been before I met Priscilla, and I realized this meant either being alone or being free to find someone else.

Looking up, I realized Priscilla was no longer in the

kitchen. Through the bay window I could see her outside, standing beside the Spanish-tile fountain. On the other side of the garden, sunshine was trickling through the bamboo grove, dappling the whole scene with a beauty that began to ease my anger. It was sad that we were fighting, that we couldn't appreciate what we had.

I went out to her to apologize.

"Sometimes, I'd like to just give it all up, Michael," she said. "My career and everything, and go live in Europe."

"We'd just be taking our problems along with us, baby. You don't want to get married, and I don't want to get married. You don't want a child, and I don't want a child."

"Michael," she said, taking my hand. But the words didn't come.

"We've become a nightmare," I said, "haven't we?"

"Perhaps we weren't ready for each other yet. Maybe if it had been another time or another place, Michael. I don't know."

I headed for the driveway and my Jeep. Priscilla followed behind me, saying nothing. I climbed in, and she stood by the passenger door. Her big blue eyes were on the verge of tears, so childlike and vulnerable, bewitching me now just as they had on that first night, many years earlier, when we'd met and fallen in love. I looked at her, my heart breaking and tears welling up in my eyes. Priscilla's lower lip was trembling. I gestured for her to come around to my side, and as she moved toward me, I could see the wet coffee stain outlining her breast. We'd had everything you could ever hope for—romance, friendship, fame, and all the fun that money can buy—and yet ours had become a twisted, tortured love affair. It was my fault. I'd lost my sense of self living behind those big iron gates, and I was no good for either of us anymore. I put my hand behind her neck, running my fingers through her long, honey-blond hair. I gently pulled her face close to mine.

"I cherish you more than you'll ever know," I said. "I'll always love you, Priscilla—you and Lisa."

I meant it.

She lowered her head to hide her face. I lifted her chin tenderly to make her look at me.

"What went wrong with us, baby?" I asked.

She closed her eyes, unable to look at me.

"I didn't believe this would ever happen to us," I said. "Why couldn't we talk?"

"We did," she said.

"No, we didn't. Not about the things that were destroying us."

"We talked more than Elvis and I ever did," she said.

Willy, our big brown pointy-nosed Doberman, came running to us. He immediately sensed our trouble and started shaking. Willy had been with us from the beginning, and I could remember the day we'd found him, a lost puppy on the roadside. We'd been on our way to Santa Barbara to drop our kids off at summer camp. Priscilla and I both had little daughters almost the same age. I'd had to stop to relieve myself, and I heard some rustling in the bushes. Out crept a little sickly bloated brown puppy with bloodshot eyes. He sat on my boot and looked up at me pleadingly. I carried him back to the girls and we decided to keep him. Priscilla was happy that her Doberman, Ninja, would now have some company.

"Ninja's getting fat and lazy," she said. "All she does is sleep all day. It'll be good for Ninja to have a puppy to play with. I only hope it doesn't give her a heart attack."

Later I learned that Elvis had been uneasy around Dobermans. After Priscilla and Elvis were divorced, and he'd found out that she'd acquired Ninja, he was upset and referred to the animal as "that devil dog."

For years, Willy was like our child, and I couldn't bear the thought of losing him, too.

I kissed Priscilla and pulled her to me. We were at an impasse, both of us hesitating to speak the truth, which was that we might be parting for good this time.

"Say good-bye to Lisa for me," I whispered. Priscilla's fears had been justified all along. My love for Lisa always bordered on intimacy. As Lisa grew to a young woman it was a constant battle for me to keep my feelings in the proper perspective. When Lisa threw her arms around me in a daughterly way and said, using one of her many pet names for me, "Merky, I love you. You're so cute," I melted. She unknowingly exuded the same power of sexual charisma that her father had wielded over millions.

I knew the time had come for Priscilla and me to say good-bye.

"You have a special place in my heart," she said. "I'll be there for you, always."

I doubted that. Past experience told me that when a man and woman part, they go in different directions. We were already on different paths, and there was no reason to believe that we would come together again. She took my face in both hands, tears running down her cheeks.

"I mean that, Michael. You must believe me."

I was thinking of the time that Priscilla had told me about Elvis calling her in the middle of the night, after they'd separated, and insisting that she get out of bed, that he was coming over.

"I have to talk to you," Elvis had said.

She'd been very upset, because the fellow she'd been involved with had spent the night with her. Elvis had argued with Priscilla in his usual persuasive manner, and she'd ended up letting him come over. She hid her boyfriend in the bedroom, and she sat with Elvis in the garden room down by the pool, talking until the sun came up, just like they used to do.

"I need you, Cilla," Elvis said. "I've never felt so alone in my life."

Priscilla asked Elvis if he wanted something to eat, or could she make him some coffee?

"No, Sattnin, I just need you to hold me close."

He'd looked awful, his hair greasy and messed up, his face puffy, and his overweight body stuffed into a dirty Esso Gas jumpsuit, and he'd been wearing old bedroom slippers.

By then, she and Elvis had gone in different directions. How hopeless he must have felt that morning, sitting there in the cabana in his rumpled jumpsuit.

Priscilla had told me how excruciating it had been to have to reject Elvis that morning. Even if she'd wanted to return to him, what about the man in her bed upstairs?

Elvis had told her he'd been up all night recording, but he'd probably been out partying and had got lonesome for his one and only true love. I hoped I'd never come crawling back to her like that. I'd found that once a woman loses her need for a man, the desire for him is gone forever.

I started the Jeep, knowing we'd said everything we could. Willy wanted to jump in with me, as he'd always done.

"What about Willy?" Priscilla asked.

I knew if I stayed another second, we'd just torment each other more and end up fighting again. "You keep him, Priscilla. He's Ninja's buddy. I can't keep a dog in my condo, and you have all this area for him to run in."

What I really wished, as I had through all our years together, was for her to beg me to stay, climb in the Jeep beside me, wrap her arms around my neck, and tearfully say that she couldn't live without me, but we had reached the end, and from now on all we could ever be was a memory.

I hugged Willy's big old head and said, "I love you, Willy." Then I drove out the gate.

I didn't want to look back but I did, and I saw her reflection in the rearview mirror. There stood my woman, my life for the past seven years. What the fuck had gone wrong? I could find all kinds of reasons to blame our breakup on Priscilla, saying it was her career, or she was unfaithful, or she'd grown cold, or she wouldn't let me be me. But they'd only be half-truths. The problem was that we'd been living in the shadow of the king. I had tried to be something that I wasn't. I'd tried to replace Elvis in Priscilla's life and in doing that had lost myself, the very thing that had attracted her to me in the first place.

In my last glimpse of her, she was struggling desperately to keep Willy from lunging after me.

1

Our military installation in Cuba is the major U.S. stronghold in the Caribbean, and a ten-foot chain-link fence topped with barbed wire is all that stands between us and Castro's Cuba. As a marine, I was stationed there during the Cuban missile crisis in 1963, and two days after my arrival, I was awakened at 4:00 A.M. by a piercing siren. We had sixty seconds to be in full combat dress and standing at attention in the street below the barracks. As we piled into the open trucks, I found out that our destination was the fence line. Overhead, U.S. fighter jets screamed into a twinkling, star-filled sky. High up on the ridge line, also heading for the fence, tanks rumbled along, their huge headlights flashing around drunkenly. Antitank vehicles armed with 106 recoilless rifles buzzed ahead of them. In the back of the speeding trucks, we held on with all our strength as the drivers raced to the fence line. Skidding to an abrupt stop, we jumped out, dug in for action, and waited.

On the other side of the fence, Cuban soldiers scattered

in panicky retreat, knowing their obsolete weapons were no defense against the bristling array we confronted them with. This was my first time to get a good look at their homeland. The Cuban landscape lay serene in the soft light of dawn, surrounded by turquoise water. I felt like an intruder violating the peaceful countryside. The fence line we'd erected was a jagged scar across their land, a symbol of the explosive relations between the U.S. and the U.S.S.R.

Forty-five minutes later an alarm sounded, ending the drill, and we began heading back to the barracks. Smoke trails were rising as the Cubans cooked their meager tortillas and beans over primitive, outdoor fires, filling the air with a scorched smell.

"I'd like to go over that fence and grab Castro's bony ass," I heard one of the short-timers curse. "I'm tired of this early morning bullshit."

All I knew of Cuba had come from reading Ernest Hemingway in high school, and my grandfather, a cigar smoker, telling me Cubans made *Romeo y Juliets*, the best cigars in the world. I'd always been drawn to the unknown and had sworn that, before I left, I'd get a better look at what was on the other side of that fence.

Fifteen months later, nearing the end of my tour of duty at Gitmo, I pulled a week of rifle-range detail. In a scuffle with another marine, I slipped down between the targets, tearing the cartilage in my knee. Soon thereafter I was ordered stateside for an operation. My last night on guard, I convinced one of the other marines on duty with me to go over the fence.

At the fence line as we prepared to climb over, he changed his mind—and I nearly did too.

"I'll watch out for you," he said, and I began climbing.

Dropping to the ground on the other side was a scary feeling, and everything I'd learned in the marines I put into practice. Running low, I made for the nearest clump of bushes. Taking cover, I looked back, and my buddy waved at me from the other side, grinning like an idiot.

Ahead, in the distance, came the sound of voices from a Cuban guard shack. Advancing across the rough terrain, I had to be careful with my knee, which had been aching since I'd jumped down from the fence. It had filled with fluid after the rifle-range accident, and I felt it swelling again.

A quick reconnaissance of the Cuban guards fast asleep in front of a low fire satisfied my curiosity, and I started back. Climbing over the fence again, I was glad to see the smiling face of my buddy.

"You crazy asshole," he said. "You were over there a long time—"

"Man, I feel sorry for those bastards," I said. "They're pitiful—sleeping in the dirt, no chairs, no radios, no shelter, just some dusty old blankets on the ground."

I'd wanted one last hurrah before leaving the marines. We'd been trained as assassins, but we never got to use our skills. At least I wouldn't be going home with nothing to brag about—now I'd had a taste of the daring associated with being a marine. Besides my fence-climbing escapade, I also helped pull two dead Cubans out of the international waterway running through Gitmo. They'd been shot by their own men while trying to swim to freedom.

Although a lot of Uncle Sam's dollars had been invested in me, and hundreds of thousands of other marines, to turn us into first-class fighters, we were nothing more than a show of power, our presence in Cuba hinting at a freedom that we weren't allowed to deliver.

I was very homesick, and wanted nothing more than to be on the next MATS flight out of there. Back in the States, I was slated for knee surgery. I'm told that to save expenses in case you die during surgery, the military puts you in the naval hospital closest to your hometown, which in my case meant Pensacola, Florida. That way, they won't have to ship your body home with an honor-guard detachment. They can just call your family and ask them which local funeral home to release the body to.

Gitmo was the climax of my disruptive four and a half years in the U.S. Marine Corps, where I'd had discipline shoved down my throat by, in my opinion, a bunch of bone-headed, aimless functionaries. Even though I'd received meritorious masts for achievement above and beyond the call of duty as off-hours captain of the water polo and swimming team at each base where I'd been stationed, I never achieved a rank above private, first class. I was constantly being busted, my promotions stripped, because I wouldn't go along with ridiculous orders and nonstop, mindless duties—scrubbing the floor with a toothbrush; painting everything that didn't move, like tree trunks, fences, and curbs; cleaning shitters and pissers, and continuously policing the area for cigarette butts, all in the name of service to our country.

I'd been in and out of trouble with authority in my hometown ever since junior high school in Pensacola. My mother and father had divorced when I was six months old. My father had left a wife, two children, and a strong-willed mother-in-law for a buxom blond Texas heiress. Like the absentee father in *The Glass Menagerie*, he'd "skipped the light fantastic out of town," never to return. The in-crowd at school snubbed everyone who wasn't from a well-to-do family, and though my mother provided the basics with her salary as a high school teacher, rich we weren't. I must have been about twelve when I started drinking, in part as a reaction to having no father and the rejection at school. But things changed with my thirteenth birthday.

My only sister, Jeannie, was sixteen and an Elvis fan. Wishing me a happy thirteenth birthday in 1957, she handed me my first Elvis album, adding that she thought I looked like him. That night, in the privacy of my room, playing the LP, I carefully studied the photographs of Elvis on the album. Looking in the mirror, I brushed the hair off my forehead, looking for similarities to Elvis. As I put the record on for the third time, I found I had mastered his every nuance—the full lips parted sensuously and the soulful eyes—and a feeling of freedom began to unfold within me. For the first time, I became aware of a depth to my feelings, and I cried and felt sad and happy all at once.

With Elvis, I learned it was possible to dream, and I knew I'd never be lonely again.

Soon I was combing gobs of Wildroot Cream Oil through my hair to look like Elvis, and I found that, almost overnight, I'd become popular with girls. I was in demand, invited to all the teenage parties, but, ironically, now I preferred being alone, spending hours in front of the bathroom mirror.

I played hooky, spending my afternoons watching *Loving You* at the Rex Theatre, slouched down in the back row, spellbound by the tough, sullen, hot-tempered character on the screen—a rebel against the system. My shop teacher refused to let me into his class until I cut my hair, which was now a well-oiled, shocking creation. He sent me to the principal, who threatened to paddle me if I didn't get it cut off immediately. I was in a predicament—I didn't want to embarrass my mother, who after all was a teacher, yet I couldn't sacrifice my hair, the symbol of my new life.

I skipped school the next day and returned to Elvis at the Rex, hoping to find an answer. I did. In the part he played, he wouldn't take anything from anybody, and the following day I found myself—and my long hair—back in the principal's office. Bent over a desktop, my trousers down and my hands grasping my ankles, I presented my bottom for punishment. As he wielded the big perforated paddle, he said, "You have until Monday to cut off that hair."

Over the weekend, I got drunk and crashed my mother's car. On Monday, the principal locked me in his office, saying he was going to get scissors to cut my hair. I smashed a chair through the window and escaped. I was expelled, and the pattern continued at the next school, and the next. Since the system wouldn't allow me to be myself, I declared war on the world and began my drift into near-delinquency. After another drinking-and-driving violation, I was threatened with jail.

I enlisted in the marines. It was 1962, I was eighteen years old, and John F. Kennedy was our president. Arriving for boot camp at Parris Island, South Carolina, I didn't argue when they led me to the barber shop and shaved my head. The recruitment billboard had said JOIN US! WE'RE LOOKING FOR A FEW GOOD MEN. But instead of becoming a good man, in the marines I became a drunk, guzzling beer and partying all night long. Drinking in the military was as routine as reveille; the requirement for eligibility into The Few, it seemed, was serious interest in two things: fighting and alcohol.

During my fifty-one months, two weeks, and three days in the marines, the corps ran my whole life, from medical and dental to daily meals and housing. The only thing they taught me was how to fight and kill. As I was approaching release into normal society at the age of twenty-two, with only these skills, it was bewildering. I hardly remembered how the civilian world functioned.

Back in my hometown, after surgery on my knee the doctors told me I'd be laid up for a month and I should stay off my leg. I wasn't about to buy that—so I sneaked out of the naval hospital every afternoon on crutches to do my regular workout, swimming a mile a day, and within a week I was strong enough to be released from the hospital. I had less than six months' enlistment left and was assigned to light duty with the marine detachment at the Pensacola Naval Air Station.

The most positive thing the corps had given me was a glimpse of the world beyond my hometown, and I regretted even the thought of returning to the old crowd with their small-town ways. During my off-duty hours, I worked part-time on Santa Rosa Island as a night clerk at a motel. I continued partying hard in all my spare time, making love with as many pretty girls as I could get my hands on.

One of my escapades lasted longer than the usual weekend affair. Her name was Grace; I liked her big breasts, her big brown eyes, and her Southern drawl. I got her pregnant and found myself with a child on the way and no means of supporting a family.

I tried conning my way into a better-paying position as manager of another motel. It was a run-down wreck of a place that was considered second-rate on the island.

"You're okay," the owner said, reeking of whisky. "But what we need is an older couple."

"No, you don't," I said. "You need someone young and strong, because this place is falling apart."

I'd sparked his interest.

"That so?" he said. "But we need a couple."

"You've got one," I said, twisting the truth a bit. "And we're expecting our first child."

"That's good," he said. "That's real good. We'd like to meet the little woman."

It was the middle of hurricane season when I told Grace about the offer. She was reluctant to take on such responsibility, and she feared the gale-force winds that fiercely battered Santa Rosa Island, causing frequent evacuations. I told her not to worry, that I was a marine, that I "wasn't afraid of nothing," and to consider it an adventure. Grace and I accepted the position at the motel, and we were married the following week. I began counting the days until my discharge.

At the end of my enlistment in the marines, I reported to headquarters. The lieutenant scribbled his signature on my release papers, and, shaking his head, handed them over to me. Because of my record, I was prepared for the worst. Besides having a history of insubordination, I'd been court-martialed for misappropriation of government property and sent to the brig for thirty days. While working in Supply, I'd helped myself to four pairs of green utility outfits, two for me and two for a buddy. Someone had seen me take them and squealed. As I accepted the papers from the lieutenant I acted nonchalant, but when I saw the word *general* where *honorable* should have been, it was a kick in the gut.

"I hope you fit in better on the outside, Edwards," he said.

I hated the feeling of desolation that was creeping over me.

"Don't take it so hard," he said. "In six months you can appeal for an honorable. Just keep your nose clean."

"That's my worry now, sir," I replied, saluting sharply.

"Stop beating your head against the wall," he said, dispensing with military protocol. "Trying to do it your way has only screwed you up."

I couldn't wait to get out of his office and be free again. In the military I'd been told to keep my mouth shut and my ideas to myself, just like I'd been treated in school. I told my new employer at the motel that I could save his failing business if he would give me free rein. For someone with nothing else in his life, the challenge of pulling this business out of the hole was just what I needed. I loved everything about running that place, from helping the revolving cast of travel-weary tourists, to repairing air-conditioners and TVs and unclogging commodes and sinks. During two and a half years of managing the motel, Grace and I made it one of the most popular places on the island. For years after, people would return, asking for me. I made them my family, and they responded to us as family, taking delight in watching our daughter, Caroline, toddling around the place.

My work at the motel was gratifying, because I was accomplishing something. But I began to get itchy. It was time for new adventure, and New York was on my mind. Grace and I had purchased a new Camaro a year earlier and we'd been asked by the Chevrolet dealer to do a test TV commercial; he was looking for "a typical couple." When the director and his crew interviewed us in the motel office, with maids, desk clerks, and pool boys bustling about, he said, "This isn't exactly what Chevrolet had in mind, but we'll film you anyway. You never know." I offered complimentary rooms, showed them the nightlife, and gave them free surfing lessons. A few days later, the director handed me his business card and said, "Thanks for the vacation, and if you're ever in Manhattan, you might try modeling. Look us up. We'll have lunch and talk."

He'd planted a seed that sprouted instantly. I was ready to leave for New York at once. Grace didn't want to go, and pleaded, "Please, don't throw this away. You've worked too hard, and they've promised us part ownership next year. Besides, don't you care about our daughter?"

"I'll be coming back a lot. Why don't you take over the motel and run it yourself—you can make a fortune."

"Caroline worships you," she said. "It'll break her heart if you leave her."

I loved my daughter and wanted to be with her but I knew I had to leave. I didn't want to miss what the world had to offer. The more experience I gained, the better my life would be, and Caroline could only benefit from my gains. I promised Grace again that I'd be coming home a lot. She didn't want to manage the place alone, so I hired a new manager, spent a month showing him the ropes, and went to New York and looked up the director.

His luncheon invitation turned out to be about as valid as the deed to the Brooklyn Bridge. When I arrived in New York, he never took my calls. I moved into the West Sixty-third Street YMCA, determined to conquer New York as I had Pensacola. I began making the rounds of modeling agencies, but no one was receptive because I had no photos. I was given a list of photographers and finally connected with one of them, who told me we'd shoot some pictures in Central Park if I could find a pretty girl to work with.

I arrived in the park early and saw a girl strolling through the zoo. We began talking and I convinced her to pose with me. When we started to work with the photographer, neither the girl nor I knew what we were doing, but the photographer assured us we were "naturals"—and I was on my way as a model. Damn, I thought, this isn't so hard.

The money I'd saved from the motel was quickly drained by what I sent home and by New York prices. I moved from the Y into a run-down third-story walkup on the West Side, sleeping on a mattress on the floor. The job I found as a dishwasher at Adam's Apple lasted exactly one week. I was too proud—I hadn't come to New York to do mess duty. I watched the busboys eating leftovers from dirty dishes. I was hungry, but I couldn't scavenge like that.

I wasn't used to big-city life, I was homesick, and I began to be unsure why I was there, without a single friend. I missed the beach, surfing, and the sunshine of Florida. My lifeline was my family—Mother, Caroline, and Grace, who I'd call when my courage waned. I hit bottom when I tried out for a porno film and was rejected as "too sullen." On my way home, I passed an elderly woman in mink, her fingers sparkling with diamonds and rubies, cleaning up after her poodle. I decided to snatch her purse. I would only take the money and somehow return her purse. I moved toward her, and her little mop of a dog attacked me. I backed off.

Then I got sick. Depression and malnutrition took their toll, and I came down with chills, fever, and nausea. I missed my daughter and wanted to go home, needing someone to hold. The big, loveless rock of a city had me terrified. Lying there in my miserable dump of an apartment, I suddenly laughed, remembering something my marine drill instructor had told us—"I'm going to turn you into one tough bunch of bastards!" I don't think he'd ever been broke and hungry in New York, though.

I was puking my guts out, and it seemed like my whole stomach was going to come up. In the middle of January, with ice and snow flying outside my window, I threw off my makeshift covers, headed to the corner deli, and bought a quart of orange juice and a large can of Del Monte fruit cocktail. On the way back, passing a bum sleeping in a phone booth curled up on the floor, I thought, That's my next stop. Looking up at the gray sky, ice stinging my face, I cried to God, "What have I done?" Just as I was about to give up, a signal went off inside me, and the do-or-die fighting spirit of the marines surfaced.

That afternoon I burst into the Ford modeling agency. I charmed one of the bookers into signing me up and ended up going home with her and having my first home-cooked meal since I'd been in New York. That night in her arms was the best I could ever remember.

My first job was an ad for Sears. I was holding a baby, and during the shoot I began to think of Caroline, realizing how much I missed her. I almost lost it.

In late March I decided to try my luck as a model in L.A. I'd heard that the Nina Blanchard Agency was willing to represent anyone from Eileen Ford's, so I left New York behind me. In my youthful innocence I was angry that I hadn't been able to conquer the city, but I swore one day I'd return and kick its ass.

2

I rented a little place just east of the Santa Monica Pier. It was smaller than the single room I'd had in New York, but if I craned my neck out the window, I could see the Pacific Ocean sparkling in the sunshine. I was happy there and looked forward to starting each day working out on the beach to restore the health and physique I'd lost in New York.

One evening while exploring my new neighborhood, I walked down below the pier. I was hungry and stopped at a food stand run by an old woman. We talked as I ate my supper of butter-drenched corn on the cob. She was a seventy-eight-year-old actress who reminded me of my grandmother and I enjoyed her company. She believed she was still a starlet and continued to paint her face with heavy stage makeup. I got a kick out of watching her argue with some drunks who came up to the stand. When she started boasting about her glorious past as La Divina, the derelicts jeered and called her names. Furious, she grabbed her ice-cream scooper and used it to flick hot butter on them. In her mind, she was still in her glorious youth and wasn't about to let anyone tell her differently.

Sitting on the end of the pier, breathing in the fresh ocean air, I felt revitalized. It reminded me of Pensacola. Even though I missed my mom and daughter, I now felt I'd made the right decision in leaving them behind.

The next day I had my interview with Nina Blanchard. I was prepared to deal with a tough cookie, since she had a reputation as a hard-boiled model's agent. When I met her, I agreed. But when I got to know her better, I found she wasn't at all the generalissimo she often portrayed in the office. Underneath the growling agent image lay a sensitive and caring woman. But the first thing she did when we met was frown at my long hair and say, "That's got to go, sweetheart, if you want to work in this town. You're not in New York now."

I hadn't caught on yet as a model, but I'd perfected a "look" for myself—an intense James Dean attitude and Elvis Presley's wild hair. I didn't agree with Nina, but I wanted to be with her agency so I told her I'd get a haircut —and that I appreciated her advice. This made her happy and contracts were drawn up for me to sign immediately. I never got my hair cut, and Nina didn't bring the subject up again.

Hollywood life suited me fine. I loved hanging out on Sunset Boulevard with another model who'd just done a surfing movie. We stood in front of the Old World Restaurant, wearing sleeveless black T-shirts and Levi's, sticking our thumbs out every time a pretty girl drove by. It was easy to make friends. Everyone had the same thing on their minds—sex and grass.

I didn't have a car, but getting around L.A. in the pre–Charles Manson 1970s wasn't a problem, and since this was the era of communes I found myself crashing on a different couch every night. I was paying my dues, as a beginning model perpetually broke and rejected by photographers. When the day came that I was so broke I had to ask my mother to pay my child support, a scary thought occurred. No one has immunity from failure. If I didn't make it here, where else was there to go? One thing I knew. No matter how bad things got, I was never going back to Pensacola. My time away from home had convinced me that the opportunities were elsewhere. And I was determined to take my daughter away from small-town life.

As I was having my lunch below the pier one day, La Divina patted me on the arm and offered me some free corn on the cob.

"Try not to get discouraged, Handsome," she chirped. "Your big break is just around the corner."

She belted out a chorus of "Somewhere Over the Rainbow," as everyone turned around and stared. That didn't bother her at all; she went right on singing. I thought she was a real nut, but there was something about her grittiness I really loved. She reminded me of Shelley Winters—she didn't give a damn what anybody thought.

On a drizzly day in June, my agent called with an interview for Johnson's Baby Oil. I was hung over and didn't want to be bothered with what I was sure would turn out to be just another rejection. As I crawled back under the covers, the phone rang again. A sweet little voice from Pensacola wished me "Happy Father's Day!" adding, "Mommy said I could call you!"

It was Caroline, and I said, "How's my baby doing?"

"Can I come and see you soon?" she begged.

"As soon as I can swing it, baby," I said, feeling a wave

of guilt. I looked around my room and added, "You'll love it here. It's right next to the water, like the motel was."

"When will your picture be in the magazines?"

"Real soon, I promise."

The call expressing her hopes was just what I needed to get my ass into town for the interview. Caroline was my whole reason for living. I knew what it was like to be disappointed as a child and there was no way I was going to disappoint her. I was going to make my daughter proud of me and when I was successful enough, I would have her come live with me and go to school in California.

At the Chateau Marmont, it seemed like every top model in Los Angeles, male and female, had gathered for this particular job, and all of them were dressed up and carrying portfolios bulging with tear sheets. I felt out of place in my jeans and T-shirt, but at the same time glad I stood out. I wasn't uncomfortable with these pro's, because I always believed that one day I'd leave them far behind. I was determined to create my own look in the modeling world, a look that no one had achieved before.

When the assistant called out my name, I strode up to him and tossed my book down on the table. After he flipped through my meager photographs, he took a Polaroid shot of me. Richard Noble, the photographer, took very little interest, saying only, "Don't you ever smile?"

"Yeah, if there's something to smile about."

"Well, do you think you could smile for me?"

I smiled as he took me by the chin and slowly moved my head, examining my face very closely.

"Thank you," he said. "You can go."

Returning to Santa Monica, I found a grocery bag of potatoes, carrots, onions, and cubes of stewing beef sitting in my doorway. The attached note read:

Good luck. I know you got it.
Your biggest and best fan,
The Vegetable Man

The Vegetable Man was a nickname I'd given to a neighbor in my building who was responsible for my not starving. He was always leaving fresh vegetables at my door, and this evening I invited him over and told him about the interview. As the stew simmered on my hot plate, he told me the story of his life—his fears, unhappiness, and frustrations—and that he envied my heterosexuality. I put my arm around his thin shoulders and said, "Maybe one day things will change for you. Anyway, I think you're great the way you are. You sure saved my ass. I'd be starving without you."

He started crying, and so did I. It was the first time I'd cried in front of another man. We took our dinner down to the beach and sat in the children's swings as we ate our stew.

Three weeks later, I landed the Johnson's Baby Oil job. It was my first all-day booking, and the fee was an astronomical $500, about $2,000 by today's standards. The ad, a double-page color spread in *Seventeen* magazine, would give me national exposure.

We shot at Zuma Beach, past Malibu, at sunset.

"You know, none of the clients wanted you," Richard said. "When I showed them your Polaroid and one of your pictures from your book, they complained you were too intense. I had a hard time getting them to accept you."

His assistant handed me a pair of cutoffs, and after I put them on Richard positioned me, having me lie on my side with my fist propping my head up, my other arm across my chest, showing off my bicep. Richard placed his Nikon on a little block of wood on the sand and, lying three feet from my face, started shooting.

"Did anyone ever tell you that you look like James Dean?" he asked.

I felt myself grinning awkwardly.

"Looks like there's a sense of humor hidden under all that moodiness. That's good. I like that. James Dean with wit."

I broke into laughter, but he told me to stop.

"Try expressing that without laughing," he said.

"Can I smile?" I asked.

"It's your shooting. You can do anything you want."

"But I can't laugh."

"Not if it's to cover up your feelings."

"I don't follow you."

"Just be yourself. Okay? I want what's inside you. Show it to the camera."

"I don't think I can do that," I replied.

"Who told you you couldn't?"

He continued shooting. "There's so much intensity and anger in those eyes," he said. "But I also see some mischief, especially when you were embarrassed and laughed a moment ago."

I wanted to turn my face away because I felt tears coming to my eyes. He was skillfully stirring up emotions I'd always kept hidden.

He peeped out from behind the camera and winked at me. "I like what I see happening to you," he said.

"I do too, I think." I was grinning now.

"There's the humor I was looking for."

He started shooting again, and I felt something fall into place inside me. All of a sudden, I had found this special world that existed between me and the camera. Power surged through me. I was able to express myself safely without having to worry about someone rejecting me. Richard was a real pro, and knew how to bring out what he wanted in the models he was shooting. His belief in me and his patience gave me the confidence I'd been struggling for. He helped me find and experience a feeling even stronger than lovemaking. I reached a place that I'd never known before. The spotlight. It felt good there.

After shooting, I got dressed and Richard and I went down to the water. He told me to be on the lookout for a sick, beached seal. On the first day he'd come to the beach on this assignment, he'd come across the seal and had been nursing it along ever since, bringing it food, but now it was gone. We stood in silence for a few minutes, looking out to sea, searching for the seal, but there was no sign of it.

We said good-bye, and Richard climbed into his car. I'd had my first taste of success that day modeling with Richard. His assistant gave me a lift back to Santa Monica. On the way home, I thought back over the shooting that afternoon and how Richard had winked at me from behind the camera. I could see by his reaction to me that I was good, that I had it. I liked the feeling and now believed that things would soon be changing for me. Richard made me feel like I really did stand a chance, after all.

A few months later, I woke up one Monday morning with the phone ringing and another hangover. This wasn't good. I didn't want my life becoming an endless procession of mornings after. My insides felt like it looked outside: gray, empty and dismal. I stumbled to the phone, polishing off a half-empty beer to stop the pounding in my head, instinctively reaching for a pencil to write down my interviews.

"Michael, have you seen your picture in *Seventeen?*"

"What picture?"

The line clicked, and Nina came on the phone.

"I think we've got something here that you'll be happy to see," she said.

An hour later, in Hollywood, as I entered the agency, everyone turned and stared at me. And then I saw the reason for their attention. Every agency has a Wall of Covers—and smack in the middle of Nina's was my double-page spread. There I was, Johnson's Baby—a bronzed, sculpted Greek god, exuding virility, eyes burning passionately, long hair wild and flowing.

"Beautiful work, darling," Nina said, rubbing my shoulder. "Just amazing. Come on into my office. We have work to do."

"The phones haven't stopped ringing," she said, sitting down behind her desk. "Everyone wants to know who's the guy in the baby-oil ad. We've already booked you for two TV commercials, and they shoot this week. I'm having to turn down offers."

"But I've never even been on an interview for a TV commercial, Nina. What do I do?"

She just looked at me for a moment. "For a while there, I thought I was going to have to take a hammer to break your shell. I was beginning to think marines have something against smiling."

I realized I was grinning from ear to ear. The door was open. I had had my first break.

When I got home, *Seventeen* in hand, I ran to the Vegetable Man's door. I wanted to show him the magazine and share my triumph, but there was no answer, and I banged harder. I tried the door; it was unlocked, and I went in. He was infected with hepatitis and told me I shouldn't come close. Sitting on the edge of the bed, I told him not to worry, I wasn't going to catch anything. He was feverish, and his face had turned an orangish color. I offered to take him to the doctor but he refused, telling me his aunt was on her way down from Bakersfield.

I showed him *Seventeen*, opened to my photo.

"I knew it," he said, somehow managing to smile. "I told you, didn't I?"

"It's not that big a deal," I said, but he was completely absorbed in the photo. I left him with the magazine and walked down to the beach. On the horizon, a storm was gathering in the sunset, painting the turbulent ocean purple and orange. I now realized that if you held firmly to your convictions and didn't give in, it was possible to get anything you went after. I was determined to become the top male model in the world. That year, 1970, was the turning point of my life.

When I asked Nina for advice, she said, "With those aspirations, you'll need to go to New York or Europe. You cannot become a major model in L.A. It just won't happen here. I don't want to lose you, though, so I hope you'll give it some thought."

The next day, Bruce Weber, a young maverick photographer, called from New York. From the moment he saw my first ad, he was determined to work with me. He saw me as "the epitomy of romance," what every girl dreamed of when she thought of her ideal man—strength, tenderness and sensitivity. And he wanted to share that with the world.

All the years of stubbornly refusing to let anyone change me or my look, including my hair, had finally paid off, and I would build a career on it for the next decade. My heroic style of unruly curls caught on immediately and was copied by models throughout the world.

I was now in the company of the best in the business—Ted Dawson, Lauren Hutton, Karen Graham, and Cybill Shepherd—headed for the top.

3

I never stopped working, appearing in national ads for Yves Saint-Laurent, Christian Dior, Cerruti, and being featured in editorial layouts in *Vogue*, *Bazaar* and *Glamour*. The ads paid best, but it was the prestige of editorial work that built your reputation. On one shooting I did for a new magazine, later called *Playgirl*, I consented to be photographed nude. The girl working with me also agreed. The editor's approach to photography was daring; he told me that he planned to create a magazine with a European look. He intended to defy the outdated taboos that most American publications held about male sexuality. His contempt for censorship appealed to my own liberal beliefs, and I admired his courage and spirit of innovation.

During the shoot, my partner and I were excited to be a part of the launching of what had been represented to us as an important breakthrough that promised to show sex with class. We did our best to create beautiful and sensual photographs in a way that had never been done before. The editor said he would be tasteful in his use of the photos and agreed to let me destroy any of the slides I didn't like.

Later, when I learned from the photographer that the real concept of the magazine was no different from any other girlie magazine, I told Nina I was furious. She was very upset and said she would find a way to stop the magazine from using the photos. Eventually she was able to get them retracted, but I had to buy them back, paying not only the photographer's expenses but the other model's fee. I was ambitious about my career, but I also felt I had the right to make certain decisions. If I didn't treat myself with respect, who would?

After one of my Bruce Weber photos appeared on the cover of Fairchild's *Men's Wear*, another brilliant young photographer sought me out. His name was Albert Watson and at the time he was carrying his two Nikons in a paper bag. Our work appeared widely, and Albert saw me in another light altogether—the hard, dark warrior, solid and indestructable—great for razor-blade ads. In my favorite Watson shot, a sunglasses ad, I'm a ruthless gangster with a toothpick in my mouth, wearing a Borsalino hat and a double-breasted suit with wide lapels. This picture won a top photo award.

Albert, who was from Scotland, told me that he believed the greatest fashion photographers were overseas. I remembered Nina's advice about New York and Europe and realized Europe was now where I belonged. In my three years in L.A., I'd gone as far as I could and was now eager for the next step in my career. Also, deep inside, I was still angry over having failed in New York. The Big Apple was still my goal. Only the best could make it there. I yearned to even the score and New York always loomed in the back of my mind. The thought of returning one day kept me hungry. Until I conquered that place, I couldn't call myself a success.

Nina contacted Askew's, a modeling agency in London, and arranged for them to represent me. I moved overseas, and within months gained a reputation as the wildest, most sought-after model in Europe. I bought a little white sports car and raced around the Continent from job to job, packing my belongings in a canvas duffel and strapping it to the back of the TR6 convertible. I led a gypsy life, and in every city from Dusseldorf and Hamburg to Barcelona, Milan, London, Paris, Helsinki, and Tangier, I had a different girl.

A successful male model becomes an expert in trickery and masquerade, conjuring illusions and sexual fantasies in his work, luring the consumer with a seductive whisper: Look at me—if you wear this underwear, or use this cologne or mouthwash, all your dreams will come true and you'll be fabulous, just like me.

Once, on a shooting in Crete for an English catalog, I wet my hair, slicked it back, and lay down on the beach in a tight Speedo swimsuit. A busload of tourists gathered, and a young woman said, "Who's he think he is, Elvis Presley?"

I wondered why she mentioned Elvis when there were so many more current personalities I could have been compared with. Then I realized the image I was using was the one Elvis had projected, and that people all over the world still remembered it—an image of sexual abandon. Image was what made people buy things, and the image I'd created over the past ten years as a model was soon to bring Elvis back into my life.

There's a stigma to being a male model. You're just another pretty face, and it began to get to me. I needed something more meaningful than stacks of tear sheets from every major magazine across Europe and thousands of dollars in every currency from each country I worked in. Having no one special to share my wealth with and no place to call home left me with an empty feeling. Loneliness was one thing that neither success nor being in the spotlight could fill. I kept in touch with Mom and Caroline by sending postcards and Polaroids of my work, but somewhere inside I still felt that wasn't enough. I would have quit modeling years earlier but, like many of my colleagues, I was addicted to the easy money and gorgeous, long-legged young girls so readily available.

I'd attained everything I'd ever wanted and yet, after five years of being a top international model, nothing satisfied me. I was at the point at which many people either turn to booze or pills. I turned to both, spending money as quickly as I made it on expensive restaurants, clothes, and hashish. In the summer, I spent the weekends in the South of France, living on a friend's yacht. I danced the nights away at exclusive clubs, always accompanied by two or three vivacious models. We were invariably the focus of attention and people would gape at my tableful of beauties. We'd be joking, laughing, acting outrageous, the girls resplendent in getups that went beyond fashion, things the normal person wouldn't even think of putting together. A designer told me he created his most successful fashion ideas from watching how models dressed up for the evening.

Sometimes just to amuse ourselves we'd invite strangers to join us. I found myself, many nights, in the back of some wealthy old Frenchman's Rolls-Royce, heading for his villa, surrounded by my harem, our host vainly dreaming of ending up in bed with one of the girls. But we always left alone, the girls sticking with me, knowing I was their survival ticket.

I was burning out fast. One evening, while hitting the casinos in Monte Carlo, something happened that disturbed me. I was in the men's room combing my hair when I noticed a lot of it falling in the basin. Running the comb through my hair again, even more came out. It sent a chill up my back. The next day, at the Monte Carlo Beach Club, I dived into the warm sea and swam out to one of the white-carpeted rafts. I climbed out of the water and looked back at the swarm of people on the beach. I didn't belong here anymore, I decided, and if I still wanted to take on New York, it was time to go back to America and do it now, while I still had hair.

In 1977, I arrived at Kennedy International with $30,000 left from the fortune I'd made in Europe, wearing my favorite white gypsy pants, Spanish espadrilles, a Basque pullover, carrying a small leather shoulder bag with a few personal belongings, and a leather jacket slung over the bag. Everything else I'd left behind, except for my car, which was on its way to the U.S. via steamer.

I felt apprehensive walking into the Ford Agency. No one seemed to notice me. Then someone called out to me and, hearing my name, all the other bookers looked up. My reputation had preceded me from Europe after all, and seeing their smiling faces, I realized New York was mine for the taking. Everyone clamored around me, excitedly looking through my photos. Through Ford's, I did major layouts for half the accounts in New York, culminating in a ten-page full-color spread for *GQ,* called "The Red Issue." Everything I wore was red, including my shoes and underwear. Hotter you couldn't get, and I was getting it all, including my first taste of cocaine.

One night, after another strenuous day of bookings, I went over to another model's home. He and I had known each other briefly in Europe, and now he was a top model in New York, gracing most of the bus stops.

"Some nights I'm so tired," I said, "even booze can't revive me."

He left the room for a minute, then returned and sat down at the table. I'd never done coke before, so I didn't know what it was when he spilled some out on the tabletop. He chopped it finely with a razor blade, then scraped it into a long line, snorting it with a rolled-up fifty-dollar bill.

"Take it," he said, handing me the fifty. "The rest is yours."

Imitating his actions, I did the coke. Within seconds, euphoria hit.

"Oooooo shit!" I said. "Whoa! That's something!"

He looked up at me and, grinning, poured out some more coke.

"Take it," he said quickly, adding, "I gotta go. I'm playing basketball tonight. We're playing the FBI."

We said good-bye. My head was a racing mess. Disoriented and confused, I was so full of energy I felt like jumping up and down and screaming. He waved at me as he drove away, and I wondered how he was able to function so well, let alone play basketball.

After that, not a night went by that I wasn't high on the stuff. I would get a stretch limo for the evening, invite another male model, two or three beautiful girls, we'd stuff ourselves at an elegant restaurant, then stay up all night dancing. With cocaine, I found I had no problem doing a full day's work on no sleep.

I had been in New York three months, and, just as it had gotten to my health the last time, I began to feel like a wreck. I held the world in the palm of my hand, and it meant nothing. I took my savings out of the Hanover Trust, which now totaled $50,000, and left town. Once again, homesick for the ocean, I headed back to L.A.

4

Nina Blanchard put me to work the minute I returned to Los Angeles. In my absence from America, clients had kept up with my career through layouts in the top fashion magazines of Europe—*L'Uomo Vogue, Linea Italiana,* and *French Vogue*—and were eager to use the sophisticated look I'd developed while abroad. I was flown to Mount Whitney to do fur coats with Lauren Hutton. She and I hit it off immediately, vying to see who could speak the dirtiest. I lost. On the way home, Bill King, the photographer, and Lauren flew coach. I told them I only flew first class and would see them in L.A. I paid the additional fare out of my pocket and during the flight took a bottle of Moet to them, saying, "I don't want you to miss out on this just because you're sitting in the back." After spending as many hours in the air as I had, flying all over the world, I figured I'd paid my dues in coach, and for as long as I could afford it thereafter, I was determined to be up front.

When I entered Priscilla Presley's life, I was at the pinnacle of my career but at the same time haunted by the voice of my conscience. I was off-balance and my value system had been screwed up by too many years in the fast lane. I needed a safe harbor where I could drop anchor and chart a new course. My introduction into the private world of the Presleys came just as I was considering moving back to Europe permanently. I knew that if I stayed in L.A. any longer, my savings, which had grown to $65,000, would quickly be wasted on the city's nightlife. I had to get away from the L.A. cocaine crowd I'd become involved with, and I dreamed of buying a little bar and restaurant somewhere along the Costa de Sol and living out my days in leisure, getting fat and having a bunch of kids with a certain Catalan beauty I'd left behind.

Priscilla Presley was giving a party, and I'd been invited to it by a mutual friend, and I couldn't resist going. I'd seen Priscilla and Elvis riding motorcycles on Sunset Boulevard a few years earlier and had remained intrigued with her ever since, saying to myself, One day I'll meet her.

The night of the party, I went over to pick up Ron Levin and told him that this was going to be my bye-bye to L.A. Ron was my best friend. He was a wheeler-dealer who several years later was murdered after getting involved with Joe Hunt in the Billionaire Boy's Club, a business fraternity of bright young men from some of Southern California's wealthiest families. We'd met at the pool of the Beverly Hills Hotel, clicked like castanets and soon were inseparable running partners. He loved to come along with me to my bookings, and we'd arrive in his black limo, both of us dressed in our linen outfits, with all the wrinkles in the right places, and sporting five-o'clock shadows. Ron and I were always up to no good, but there was one big difference between us. He didn't drink or do drugs. He loved to sit back and watch everyone else do them, though. He tried to get me to invest my earnings in his financial schemes, bragging about his dealings with Muhammad Ali. When he told me Ali was careless with money, I felt bad, being a great fan of Ali's. I would have loved meeting Ali, but I decided not to ask Ron for an introduction, knowing that he might try to use this later to get something out of me. We all have a reckless side, the side that can destroy us, and my instincts told me that Ron's was money and never to get involved with him in any kind of business dealings.

On my way to Ron's, I'd stopped at Turner's liquor store and picked up three bottles of $100 French wine, having learned from experience that just because a party was in Beverly Hills, it didn't mean they'd have good wine. I seldom had hangovers in Europe and knew it was because people there didn't drink rotgut like they did over here. Sitting in Ron's living room, sipping my wine while he was getting ready, I dumped half a vial of coke on the coffee table and made myself a footlong line. I snooted and tooted until I was gnashing my teeth and teetering on the edge of the couch. When Ron came out and saw my condition, he looked amused.

"Are you going to do all that at once?"

"I'm testing my endurance," I said. "After tonight, I'm quitting. I'm not hooked on it like everyone else in this town."

Ron just gave me one of his who-do-you-think-you're-kidding looks.

Walking into Priscilla's party later that night, I was filled with anticipation. The party looked like something out of the 1950s. The girls were decked out in above-the-knee, low-cut, tight-fitting dresses, and the guys had slicked-back hair and long, painted-on sideburns. A deejay was spinning records, and memories of my boyhood began to stir. I remembered wiling away long afternoons in a Pensacola juke joint, listening to Elvis croon, "I Want You, I Need You, I Love You" and "Don't Be Cruel." As a teenager, I'd fantasized myself as Elvis, living his life in Hollywood, and finding my dream girl there.

Tonight, I had one burning desire—to meet the mysterious hostess, Elvis's ex-wife, but she was nowhere in sight.

"Where does her taste come from," Ron said, looking around the room. "Tijuana?"

He was seeing the burnt-orange carpet, chunky wooden furniture embedded with heavy iron studs, and Elvis's piano, stained lime green.

"This is really *his* style," Ron went on, but I saw it differently, noticing Priscilla's tasteful collection of paintings and antiques—an Asian shoe-shine stand with brass and chrome handles and drawers with pictures of semi-nude belly dancers; a nineteenth-century Russian samovar, and a delicately carved swan cradle overflowing with cut flowers.

Joe Esposito, Elvis's road manager, greeted us, commenting on the fact that I was carrying my own bottle of wine and one of Ronnie's Baccarat glasses, which I was already drinking from.

"You guys hungry?" Joe asked. "There's a nice spread of eats and stuff set up in the dining room. Help yourself!"

This wasn't the kind of party Ron and I had anticipated. We were expecting heavy-duty rock 'n' rollers. In this crowd, they were nowhere apparent. I looked around the room, searching for Priscilla, and Ron said, "Maybe she's in the kitchen, chopping cold cuts."

We invaded the kitchen and were confronted by the butler and his wife.

"We're looking for Ms. Presley," I said, taking out my cocaine and offering the butler some.

He stiffened visibly and refused.

"Send Priscilla a letter," Ron said. "Let's go."

"We're not going till I meet her," I said, walking away and leaving Ron in the kitchen with the help.

And then I saw her. She was standing across the room by the antique swan cradle, smiling and laughing with three handsome young men. She was much smaller than I'd imagined, and even though this was her house and her guests, she somehow looked out of place. I thought it was amazing how she was able to give the guys flirting with her such rapt attention and at the same time, without their knowing, keep an eye on the door for new arrivals. She seemed very confident, and at first I thought she was on the prowl and really enjoying herself. But then I sensed something else. It was possible she still wasn't over Elvis, and she was filled with desperation. I moved closer for a better view and then she saw me.

"I'm Priscilla," she said, looking at me with interest. "I haven't danced with you, have I?"

"Not yet," I said.

She held her hand out to me, and we shook hands. Looking into her eyes, I was overwhelmed. As a model, I'd been involved with many beautiful women, but Priscilla possessed something more than beauty, and it's called allure. I took her in my arms, and we became the center of attention on the dance floor. She had a curvy little body, daringly revealed by her costume, and her full lips were painted bright red. As we danced, I held her so close that only our clothes were keeping us from making love. She held on to me as if she couldn't get close enough, communicating more confidently with her body than she had with words. I looked into her blue eyes, and they seemed to be saying, "Do anything you want to me, I'm yours." My stomach grabbed hold of itself inside, making me feel emotional for her. I was aroused and wondered if she was experiencing the same overpowering feeling.

"Where are you from?" she asked.

"L.A. But I lived in Europe the last five years."

"I thought you were European when I saw you come in. What did you do there?"

"Modeled, traveled all over and enjoyed life."

"What brought you back?"

"My hair."

She looked at me strangely.

"I had a frantic schedule, and was always in planes and eating crazy. Things finally caught up with me and my hair started falling out."

She ran her fingers through my hair and said, "It's beautiful and full now."

"It settled down since I came back home," I said.

I loved her hands on me. They felt sexy, and I was glad I'd washed my hair that night.

"I've always loved traveling," she said. "In fact, I have a trip planned to New Guinea next month. I'm going to visit the cannibals. Some of the tribes still practice shrinking heads."

We both started laughing, and though the record the deejay was playing was Donna Summer's "Last Dance," we didn't stop when it was over. Priscilla raised her finger to the deejay, saying, "One more song."

I glanced around the room to see if Ron was watching us,

and I could have sworn I saw Elvis, standing back in the corner. It was his eyes, and they were fixing me with an eerie stare. For a moment I lost my step; I had to look back and see who that was, but she was gone.

5

I woke up fully dressed on an oversized suede couch in Priscilla's living room. Searching for my shoes, I found that someone had placed them beside a neat pile of little hand-made pillows. My thoughts were still reeling from a night-mare I'd had. In that dream, Elvis and I had fought over my dancing so suggestively with Priscilla.

"You're not her husband any more," I yelled. "It's none of your business how she dances now."

His familiar sneer began to grow larger and larger until his lip covered his whole face. Raucous laughter trumpeted from the cavern his mouth had become, and then he roared, "You're close to stepping in some shit, boy, and it's deeper than you think."

I pondered my nightmare and Elvis's strange warning. Dreaming about him didn't surprise me at all, after the fifties party and the feeling I had of Elvis being everywhere in this place. I rubbed my head, feeling groggy, and swore I'd never do cocaine again. Looking around the living room and into the den, I noticed that the servants must have cleaned the place that morning while I was still passed out. The house was quiet and nobody seemed to be at home. My mind remained in a fog until I saw a gardenia on the pillow. Then the evening came tumbling back to me. I remembered Priscilla and I had gone outside to the garden after dancing. She'd cut some gardenias, and she must have put one beside me while I slept on the couch.

I went outside to the pool, and as I swam I remembered the rest of the night. After the party I'd taken Priscilla to Ron's house, where I'd immediately told Ron to go to bed. I'd opened a bottle of Pouilly Fumé and we'd made ourselves comfortable in the living room. She'd confided that she wanted to be a model but felt that she was "too short."

"Nina Blanchard told me that," she said.

I laughed and pulled her close to me, whispering in her ear, "Don't pay any attention to what Nina said."

I started to kiss her on the neck, but she was more interested in talking about modeling. At that moment I realized that there was a lot more going on in her pretty little head than she was revealing. I was impressed and looked at her a little differently. I told her, "You're too beautiful to be worrying about height, and if you're really that serious about being a model, I'll get you with Nina."

"You would go to that trouble when you don't even know me?"

"I'd do a lot more than that," I said, "if you'll let me."

Later, while driving Priscilla back to her home from Ron's, I decided I wasn't leaving her that night and purposely misplaced my car keys.

"Have you checked all your pockets?" she asked, not realizing what I was up to.

"Yes. It's just that all that cocaine has gotten to me."

"I have to sleep, Michael," she said, getting me a fur

throw from a closet. "You can sleep in the living room if you like."

She turned and headed for her bedroom but I went after her, surprising her from behind and enveloping her in the fur, pulling her down on the fiery orange carpet. I wanted to kiss those full red lips and caress the voluptuous hips that my hands had ever so gently sampled while dancing. Priscilla smiled provocatively up at me, but as I pulled her close I heard someone in her bedroom.

"My girlfriend stayed the night over," she explained, as she got up and went into her bedroom, closing the door softly behind her.

I finished my morning swim and the butler came down to the pool, carrying a breakfast tray and a towel for me. I asked him where Ms. Presley was, and he informed me that she'd left much earlier that morning for an appointment, adding, "There's a shower and toiletries in the bathroom next to the pool. If you need anything else, dial three on the phone to ring the kitchen."

I felt very much at home and, wrapped in a towel, I eased back on the lounge chair to enjoy the hot midmorning sun and my breakfast. The tray included a fruit plate consisting of papaya, kiwi, bananas, grapes, and watermelon, and there was also toast, jelly, peanut butter, bacon, and scrambled eggs. My tray also included a gallon of steaming coffee in a silver thermos decanter and a big pitcher of milk. It was a marvelous breakfast and I ate every bit of it. Later on, Priscilla would tell me that Elvis had loved huge portions of food put before him at mealtime.

As I sat and stuffed myself, I imagined that this was how Elvis must have lived, lounging by the pool with Priscilla and feasting on his favorite things. No wonder he got so fat. I dozed off and the nightmare came back to me, and there before me, hovering over the pool, was a very big Elvis. All of his molecules were separating and expanding. It looked to me like he was having an out-of-body experience. As he floated up into the blue sky, he grew enormous.

"This is how God feels and sees things," Elvis said. "This is what it's like to be God."

I realized Elvis's spirit had never left. Priscilla and Lisa were still under his protection, and Elvis was waiting for the right someone to come along.

I woke up with a start. Looking up at the house, I saw a curtain fall back into place. Someone was watching me from behind a window. I wondered how long they'd been staring at me.

I carried the breakfast tray back up to the house. The couple were working in the kitchen, and the woman got flustered when, still wrapped only in the towel, I gave her a big hug, thanking her for breakfast. I asked them to tell Priscilla that I'd call that afternoon, and then I got dressed and left.

Later, at home in my high-rise apartment on Doheny, I showered and changed into fresh clothes, then headed over to Ron's with the top of the 450SL down, letting the wind and sun clear my head. I thought about my nightmare, trying to give it some meaning. It was beginning to seem like a message from above. For the past ten years I had been caught up in a world of instant gratification—cars, clothes, women, traveling, money, fine food, liquor and drugs. I believed there was a God, but I'd been too busy and too obsessed with my physical senses to be in touch with him, except in emergencies.

When I was a little boy, I loved going to church with my mother and big sister, Jeannie. The three of us would hold hands through the whole service, and I felt safe and protected. We were Episcopalians, and as the mahogany organ moaned out "Onward, Christian Soldiers," I had my first spiritual awakening. Above the organ was a life-sized crucifix, and if I stared at Jesus long enough he came to life and smiled at me. I was filled with a warm feeling of love and understood the meaning of the words "My cup runneth over." But that all changed when my grandmother converted to Christian Science. She was a domineering woman who ran the family with an iron fist and insisted that we follow her way of thinking.

Grandma was also a woman ahead of her time, an independent thinker. She'd never let anything get her down, even her glass eye, which she'd had since suffering glaucoma in her youth. She was the backbone of the family, and to get away from her busy schedule, she found a place of refuge up in the attic, reading Aristotle, Plato, and Socrates, searching for the meaning of life and filling little notebooks with her findings. She loved Grandpa, but she loved her independence just as much.

Even though she adored me, when I was about fourteen she once grabbed me by my hair and shook my head, saying, "You and that Elvis Presley hair! Is that all you think about? Always combing it! You'll turn out to be a good-for-nothing just like him."

Late one night, she fell through the trapdoor and down the attic stairs, breaking her leg. Although it was a compound fracture, she stubbornly refused a doctor, and instead followed her religious beliefs. She had us summon a Christian Science practitioner to pray for her recovery. I listened all night as he talked to her, citing over and over the Christian Science creed of "mind over matter." Finally, in the early hours of the morning, he insisted upon medical treatment but it was too late. I saw Grandma bleed to death, and I lost my faith. Our family fell apart, too, because she'd been the force that held us together, and I blamed it all on religion.

But now, racing down Doheny Drive in the Mercedes, remembering my dream of Elvis, I realized that something must have fallen into place again that morning at Priscilla's house, and I felt a resurgence of spirituality. It was a definite message—Elvis was beckoning to me. He was telling me that it was time for him to go. Even though I'd just met Priscilla, I knew in my bones that we were destined to be together. Our paths crossing hadn't been by accident.

Suddenly in the rearview mirror appeared a big black Jeep, towering above the Mercedes and bearing down on me. At the stoplight at Santa Monica Boulevard, I looked back. There behind me was an extraordinary sight. The girl in the Jeep was dressed in black, with wild raven hair streaming behind her, and her reflecting sunglasses were shining like the chrome-laden Jeep. I got out of the car and walked back to her, immediately recognizing Cher. When I inquired where she'd bought her Jeep, she replied in a husky growl, "At the Jeep place, sweetie!" Undaunted by an irate motorist blowing his horn, I waved him by and carried on with Cher, admiring her new Jeep. She told me where I could buy one and I asked her if she'd go riding with me sometime.

"You can call me," she teased. "But I've got a boyfriend."

I winked at her and returned to my car.

I made up my mind. If I was going to do Elvis's bidding, I needed a new image—and this big black mother of a Jeep was a perfect place to begin.

6

I pulled up to Ron's house on Peck Drive in Beverly Hills and sat in the driveway for a moment, considering what to do about Ron and a Nina Blanchard model (I'll call her Maggie) I'd become involved with. I wanted Priscilla all to myself and wasn't ready to share her with anyone, even Ron, whom I loved like a brother. He'd be hanging around day and night, interfering and manipulating, just as always, and causing trouble between Priscilla and me. As for Maggie, giving her up would be painful but the idea of taking Elvis's place in Priscilla's life was too tantalizing for me to let go of. I'd do whatever it took to win her heart and never let her slip away. I seized the opportunity head-on, blindly going after the crown, throwing all caution aside in my desire to be the successor to Elvis. I could already feel the power growing inside me. As I reached for his scepter Priscilla became even more desirable, and I could already see myself living as Elvis had, like a king, with Priscilla by my side.

Ron greeted me in the dining room, and, as usual, started prying.

"So what's Elvis's wife like in bed?" he asked.

I went into the den to avoid him. He followed me, asking, "Was she any good, Mikie? Elvis wasn't, you know."

"It's none of your fucking business, Ron."

"She has the softest lips."

"Don't give me that shit. You didn't kiss her."

"You're right, I didn't. She kissed me."

"When?"

"When you weren't looking, asshole."

I didn't know what his game was, but I knew he was having fun, provoking me.

"I can tell she liked me by her wet lips. When women kiss you with wet lips—"

I grabbed him by the shoulders and shoved him across the room. He sailed backward, sending papers and pencils flying, and crashed onto his leather sofa. He lay there for a second without moving, and I was afraid I'd hurt him. Then he opened his eyes and grinned.

"I bet Elvis liked her wet lips on him," he said.

I leapt on Ron and got him in a headlock. We wrestled on the sofa like two feuding brothers, neither one of us willing to give up. Then the son of a bitch grabbed me by the balls.

"You won't be much good to Priscilla without these," he chortled.

I could never win, playing games with Ron. He was too clever, and I hated all the bullshit involved in game-playing anyway. I released him, and he let go of me and jumped up.

"It's the madness," he said, going into the bathroom.

He returned with a vial of vitamin B that had a syringe sticking out of it.

"Drop your pants," he said. "You need a poke with this. That woman has brought the madness out in you."

As he stuck me with the needle, he added, "You should be making babies with Maggie. If you're not careful, you'll break her precious little heart."

Ron and I had brought this beautiful nineteen-year-old into our brotherhood some months ago. Maggie was a willowly, green-eyed blonde, with skin like tightly stretched cellophane. We'd talked about having a little boy together and moving far away from Hollywood to some remote island where we could walk naked along the beach. But that picture with Maggie was fading for me now. I'd met Priscilla.

Ron pulled the needle out and slapped me on the ass.

"Priscilla is more suited to my personality," Ron boasted. "She's ambitious, manipulating, and calculating, like me. She'd outgrow you and drop you, just like she did Elvis. She couldn't do that to me. We're both ruthless."

I'd never heard Ron talk like this before, and my first thought was, He's conning me—he wants her for himself. But something else told me he was coming from the heart. He'd once said I was the brother he'd always wanted and never had. But Ron was such a total misfit, I never knew what to believe.

He laughed and squirted the rest of the vitamin B into the air.

"If I had to choose between Priscilla and Maggie, I wouldn't hesitate. Maggie cherishes you for who you are. Priscilla will only use you."

I remembered the night before, when Priscilla and I were on Ron's couch, and I was trying to be romantic. She seemed more interested in the fact that I could help her become a model than in me.

"You've fucking lost your mind, man," I said to Ron. "I'm listening to this shit and actually starting to believe it. I'm beginning to think I'm as crazy as you. Priscilla isn't like that. She's more like me than you know."

There was something to what Ron said. It would be foolish to leave Maggie, who really loved me, for Priscilla, who seemed more interested in my image than in me. But nevertheless, as I sat there, I realized I wasn't ready to give up Hollywood and the world I'd had a glimpse of last night for the family Maggie wanted to start with me. Convinced that I could make Priscilla mine, I now had to choose between her, a sparkling diamond, and Maggie, a handful of rich, fertile earth. My heart told me to stay with Maggie, but my ego wouldn't let me give up Priscilla.

Once again I was a young man on the move, looking for something the world seemed to offer but never delivered. I was continually leaving friends and loved ones behind in my restless search. I'd left my wife and daughter. Now I was leaving Maggie.

7

Maybe my restless search was over. Maybe this time the world would deliver. I called Priscilla to invite her for dinner the next evening, but she told me she was busy.

"Change your plans," I said.

She told me she couldn't—she was treating Lisa Marie and one of her little friends to an amusement-park outing, but after a quarter of an hour of using all my persuasive powers, I talked my way into going with them. I was learning that the easiest way to change Priscilla's mind about anything was to convince her that there'd be a lot more fun doing it my way.

That evening I stood at Priscilla's front door, wondering if she'd be as attractive to me as she'd been the night before. She came to the door in tight-fitting white pants, and I had my answer. At the party she'd worn her hair in braids, but now it was down and long, and she was wearing hardly any makeup. I liked what I saw.

Standing next to her, trembling, was a sleek, black Doberman.

"You can pet her," she said, stroking the dog's head. "Ninja won't hurt you."

I put out a cautious hand but withdrew it instantly when the dog lunged at me with its nose.

"Sit, Ninja," Priscilla said, and the dog obeyed her. I reached out and this time Ninja let me pet her.

"She doesn't see many strangers," Priscilla explained.

"Yeah, she seems a little excited."

"Dobermans are very misunderstood. It's only when people mistreat them that they become mean. Ninja's really very gentle."

"What does her name mean?"

She led me inside, explaining that ninjas were Japanese hired assassins who dressed in black and moved with speed and grace, and that her involvement in karate had given her the idea of naming her dog after them.

"I think you're familiar with the living room," she said, smiling. "I won't be but a minute."

Back on the suede couch, I paged through a book on the coffee table. It was a collection of paparazzi shots, and about halfway through it I came to a wedding picture of Elvis and Priscilla. It had been so long since I'd seen the photo that I'd forgotten they were look-alikes with jet-black hair. Priscilla looked like the perfect bride, radiating love, and Elvis looked stoned, staring into space.

I heard laughter coming from the far end of the hallway and, looking up, saw two giggling girls. As they came closer I couldn't take my eyes off the cute one in T-shirt and shorts, who was obviously Elvis's daughter. She smiled shyly when she saw me, and I recognized the same haunting look on her face that I'd seen on the mystery girl at the party the night before. Lisa, almost eleven years old, wore her hair in braids and copied everything her mother did, both in dress and manners.

They paused at the huge antique postmaster's desk across the room, pretending they had some interest there, but it was clear from their whispering, giggling, and curious glances that they were checking out Mommy's new boyfriend. I was just as curious about Lisa as she was about me. As I watched her playing, I began to see her uncanny resemblance to Elvis. Every expression that crossed her face was his. It was as if his head had been placed on her body.

Priscilla's "minute" turned out to be an hour, and by the time we piled into her white Mercedes, it was 9:00 P.M. We were on our way to Magic Mountain amusement park in Valencia, California.

We went on all the rides, Priscilla and the kids screaming and flailing their arms and hanging on to me for dear life. After the Spin of Death, I went behind a tree and threw up the beer I'd drunk.

"Are you okay?"

I looked up and saw Lisa.

"Mommy told me to ask if you're okay."

"Yeah, I'm better now. Thanks, Lisa."

"We're going on the roller coaster. Do you want us to wait for you?"

"No thanks," I said, laughing. "I'll sit this one out."

I watched Priscilla and the girls climb onto the ride and, for the first time since childhood, I felt joy. I could hear the sound of carousel music coming from somewhere down the midway, and I knew this was how I'd always wanted my life to be. I didn't have to be doing wild or crazy things to be happy. This was real. I didn't want to lose it.

It was going on 2:00 A.M. by the time we returned to Priscilla's house. Lisa and her friend had fallen asleep in the car, and now a quick kiss from Priscilla sent them off to bed. I followed her into the kitchen, and she offered me some cold watermelon. She carefully cut one big slice and placed a single fork on the plate.

"Aren't you having any?" I asked.

She shook her head, and I could tell she was hinting for me to eat my watermelon and go.

"Have a little piece," I said. "It's more fun eating with you."

She cut a delicate sliver for herself and joined me.

"I'd better check on the girls," she said.

"I'm sure they're already asleep," I said. I wanted her to myself for the rest of the evening, and I prayed the girls were really asleep. Otherwise, I knew I wouldn't get anywhere with her.

I had designs of my own, and they didn't include the children—or sleeping on the couch.

When I finished my watermelon I started to get more but she took my plate, and hers, and started rinsing them. Obviously she knew what I was up to. I went up behind her, reached around and shut off the water. She turned, looking up in surprise, but before she had a chance to say anything, I lifted her into my arms and carried her from the room.

"My hands are still wet," she said.

"Use my shirt." I gripped her tighter and moved in the direction of the bedroom.

In the hall, I had to stop and balance her on my knee in order to open the bedroom door. As I turned sideways to get through the doorway, I glanced to my left. There in the hall was an antique cabinet with beveled glass, and reflected in it was a pedestal that held Elvis's gold-framed sunglasses with the big EP in the middle of them. It was very unsettling, and I kicked the door shut behind us.

As we approached her bed, she whispered, "Just a minute." At the far end of the room there were two leaded-glass doors made from old church windows, and she disappeared behind one of them. I undressed, removed a stack of lace pillows from the bed, and climbed under the sheets. I waited for what seemed an eternity. When she finally reappeared, she was freshly showered, had redone her makeup, and her breath hinted of Spearmint gum. I was astounded. She was presenting herself to me for approval, like a child earnestly offering a toy. I wanted to smile and tell her she didn't have to do that—it was unnatural. But then I realized Elvis must have forced this ritual on Priscilla, and to her it was completely normal.

I took her in my arms and our lips met softly. I pulled her teddy down off her shoulders, revealing her breasts. They were as firm as a teenager's and fuller than they looked when she was dressed. I wanted to stare at them forever. She moaned as my fingers came in touch with her.

Suddenly the sound of a loud gurgle erupted from my watermelon-bloated stomach.

"Are you all right?" she asked.

"I think so. Let me just catch my breath for a minute."

"Me, too," she said.

I'd wanted to have an evening of perfect lovemaking. But I was in distress, fighting the urge to throw up for the second time that evening. I was so sick I couldn't even sustain an erection. I thought I'd lost the one chance I had of winning her, and to make matters worse I was falling for her—hard.

"I'm sorry, Priscilla. I have to lie still for a minute."

She touched my face and said, "There's no rush."

She kissed me tenderly on my forehead, nose, and cheeks, and as she reached my lips, I fell asleep in her arms.

8

The next thing I was aware of was the aroma of fresh coffee and Priscilla's cheerful greeting, "Good morning!" After handing me my coffee she pulled the drapes wide open, letting the bountiful California sunlight flood into the room. "Isn't it a beautiful day, Michael?"

"When did you get up?" I asked. "I didn't even hear you get out of bed."

"Of course you didn't. You were snoring!"

"I don't snore. Do I?"

"You snored last night."

"Why didn't you shake me or something?"

"I didn't want to wake you up. You looked so peaceful."

"You mean you were lying there looking at me?"

"Yes."

When I asked her to go out with me that night for a quiet dinner, she accepted, adding that Lisa was going to be at her grandparents, the Beaulieus, who lived in Brentwood. I couldn't believe Priscilla wanted to see me again, after the fiasco of last night.

All that day I found myself yelling wild cries of joy and I couldn't wipe the grin off my face. Priscilla had no idea what was in store for her. At dinner I was careful with my drinking, making sure that nothing would get in the way of the evening that lay ahead of us. That night we made love until dawn.

As usual when you meet someone new, you have a tendency to ignore your old friends. I became preoccupied with Priscilla, my new girlfriend, and fell out of touch with Ron Levin for a few days. When Ron and I finally did get together again, meeting for a drink at the Polo Lounge, he was so relentlessly inquisitive about her that he made me jealous. I came up with a way to get him off my back and keep him away from Priscilla. I demanded that he give me $25,000 in cash if he wanted to be involved with us.

Without a blink, he agreed, saying, "You've got a deal."

Ron was very tight with his money, and I didn't believe he was serious. I felt sure he was bluffing and forgot all about the deal. A few days later he invited me and Maggie to dinner. We went to my favorite restaurant, the Holiday House in Malibu. Since meeting Priscilla, I was finding it increasingly difficult to be with Maggie. I didn't like deceiving her.

After we ate, Maggie excused herself to go to the ladies' room. As soon as she left the table, Ron plopped down a Security Pacific bank envelope in front of me. I recognized the unmistakable feel of a lot of money.

I opened the envelope and dumped the contents on the table. Out tumbled $25,000 in every conceivable denomination short of dimes and quarters. I piled the bills into a high stack in the middle of the table, indifferent to the other diners' curious stares.

Maggie returned and promptly covered the money with a napkin.

"What's going on?" she asked.

"I just bought something from your boyfriend," Ron said.

Maggie looked at me inquiringly.

"I can't believe you took me seriously," I said. "I don't want your money."

"You offered her to me."

"Who?" Maggie asked. When neither Ron nor I responded, she said, "Are you talking about me?"

"You tell her," Ron taunted, filling our wineglasses.

"Shut up, Ron," I said, hitting the table so hard with both fists that it went all crazy and lopsided. The money cascaded to the floor, along with our dishes, silverware, glasses, flowers, and bottles.

Completely unruffled, Ron snapped his fingers at a waiter and ordered another bottle of wine, adding, "Prop this table up with something. And hand me that money."

He sat there smiling, sizing me up, and waiting for my next move.

I suddenly realized what Ron was really after. He wasn't trying to steal Priscilla from me; he wanted to get his hands on her money.

He didn't waste any time. I knew Ron was a con man and a part-time freelance journalist and was somehow connected with a big Beverly Hills law firm. But what I didn't know, until the trial for his murder several years later, was just how scheming Ron actually was. He'd managed to play a $13-million hoax on shrewd, well-educated Joe Hunt, head of the Billionaire Boys' Club, and on an entire brokerage house. Ron then vanished in the summer of 1984 and his body was never found. Joe Hunt was tried for Ron's slaying and sentenced to life in prison without parole.

A few days after dinner with Ron and Maggie at the Holiday House, Priscilla and I were having tea down by her pool when she told me she was concerned about Ron. He'd been appearing at her house unannounced almost every day. He wanted to help her with her finances and had already proposed various investments. Some of them made good sense to her. She found Ron to be very sharp and wondered how I'd feel if she put him in touch with her accountants.

I was panicky. Ron had been staking her out. I'd never imagined he would go behind my back or move this fast.

"Is Ron Levin trustworthy?" Priscilla asked.

"No," I said. "He's not."

I couldn't believe it. Ron was at it again, flaunting his bright, many-faceted mind, like I'd seen him do so many times, using it as a magnet to draw in the unwary. Before, I'd always been amused, watching him operate, but now he was hitting too close to home. I called him and told him that he and I were through and to keep away from Priscilla if he knew what was good for him. He just laughed and said, "You'd better be worrying about yourself," and hung up.

It wasn't as easy breaking off with Maggie. After making love one night, I told her about Priscilla. She cried and said she knew it had been too good to last, adding, "If she makes you happier, I won't stand in your way. I want what's best for you."

I walked Maggie down to her car, feeling shattered. It was like acid had been poured into my heart. As she drove off down Doheny, I somehow knew I was doing something that years later would return to haunt me.

The Fourth of July weekend was coming up, and Priscilla accepted my invitation to go white-water rafting on the Stanislaus River. I'd just got my brand-new CJ5 black

Jeep, and was looking forward to showing it off to her. She told me she loved traveling and would drop anything to go adventuring. I was excited at the prospect of spending a whole weekend together, and the backdrop was going to be a beautiful wilderness area in Northern California. A makeup girl I'd met on a fashion shoot was marrying a stuntman, and they were having a big western-style wedding at Angel's Camp on the Stanislaus.

I was deliberately an hour late picking up Priscilla, who'd expected me at 7:00 A.M. I didn't want to seem too easy to get. Finally, she called me and asked if we were still going.

"You really want to go?" I said.

"Yes," she said, sighing in exasperation. "I've been waiting in the driveway for an hour."

"I'll be right over," I said.

Every instinct told me the way to keep this woman was not to be easy or predictable. In actuality, I was already dressed and had everything packed and sitting by the door. I got to her house in fifteen minutes.

I was an old hand at roughing it and had dressed appropriately—beat-up blue jeans, boots, and an old leather jacket. Priscilla was standing by her Mercedes wearing a pretty summer dress, her hair radiant, looking like she was headed for a picnic.

"We're going up to rough country," I warned. "You might mess those up, baby."

She got the idea, kicked her sandals off right there and ran back into the house and changed into a light-blue jumpsuit. Thoughtfully, she brought out a bottle of Mouton Cadet, knowing I loved wine, and I placed it in the cooler alongside two six-packs of beer and a couple of bottles of St. Emilion.

Before we took off, I popped open a can of beer for each of us. She was hesitant to drink in the morning, saying she'd never done it before, but I insisted, pointing out that it was a holiday weekend and that made it okay. Priscilla toasted me, saying, "To an exciting time—filled with lots of new adventure." Then she dug into her pocket and brought out a container of cocaine.

"This is for you," she said. "Someone gave it to me. It's been in my drawer for a long time."

I was in heaven. Using the little spoon attached to the lid, I scooped out a couple of hits. We roared out of Beverly Hills in my black Jeep, the top down, the cooler full of wine and beer, and the stereo blaring. Priscilla was grinning in absolute delight, looking mischievous and radiant as she drummed the top of her beer can with scarlet fingernails. I leaned over and gave her a big wet kiss.

We made it as far as Malibu when I saw a highway patrolman spin around behind me and come chasing after us. We'd been drinking since we'd left her house, and I had no intention of getting busted. I sped toward the hill in front of us and as soon as we dropped out of the patrolman's sight, I said, "Brace yourself," and careened into a beach colony driveway near Point Dune.

I drove into an empty garage and pulled the door down behind us. Priscilla was grinning.

"You liked that, didn't you?" I said, as she nodded happily.

In her protected, high-profile life with a rock 'n' roll superstar, I knew she'd never had to worry about running from the cops. When I felt it was safe again, we got back on the road and proceeded on toward San Francisco and the Stanislaus.

9

The directions I'd been given were so fouled up that we didn't arrive at Angel's Camp until three in the morning, ready to drop. We'd completely missed the sunset wedding. With the halogen lights mounted on the Jeep, I was able to spot everyone's tents scattered around the grounds and all that was left of the camp fire, a thin column of smoke. The Jeep's four-wheel drive enabled us to bump over the shrubs and gullies and park by the smoldering fire. From all the empty liquor bottles, beer cans and party debris strewn about, it looked like we'd missed quite a celebration last night.

We made ourselves a comfortable nest, zipping our sleeping bags together. Crawling in and getting cozy, we lay there under the stars, looking at the glowing embers of the dying camp fire and listening to the sounds of farm animals nearby.

"I'm so happy," Priscilla whispered. "I've never slept outdoors before."

"You led a pretty sheltered life with Elvis, didn't you?"

"When it comes to things like this, I guess I did."

"Are you ever afraid, being on your own now?"

"I'm more worried that Lisa doesn't have him anymore."

"Yeah, I feel guilty that I'm not raising my daughter."

"How are you handling it?"

"By writing letters, phone calls, and visiting as often as I can. She's more like a little sister to me than a daughter. We share everything, and I think she feels secure with me."

"I want Lisa to grow up to be normal and healthy and not think that because of who she is she doesn't have to do anything with her life."

We shared the last beer, and as we were drifting off a gruff voice startled us awake. A few feet away, a rugged-looking cowboy stood up and assumed the unmistakable stance of a man about to take a leak. Leaning precariously over the fire, he let out a stream that sizzled and smoked.

Priscilla sat up, alarmed. "He's going to fall in that fire," she said.

I jumped out of the sleeping bag, naked, and grabbed the cowboy just as he was about to topple into the hot coals. When I pulled him back he locked his arm around my neck, leaning on me and continuing to pee. Finally the well went dry, and he put himself back inside his fly and slurred, "Gimme a beer."

He smelled like a brewery. "Go back to sleep," I said, easing him to the ground, where he started snoring immediately.

A few hours later, at daybreak, I heard the cowboy stirring again, and this time I saw that he had a buddy with him. They were squatting nearby looking at our clothes, which we'd left by the sleeping bag when we'd undressed.

"Look," the big one declared in a raspy voice. "Their

laundry's out. They must be bare-assed in that sleeping bag."

When they realized I was awake, they brought me a big plastic cup of beer. I was never one to turn down a cold beer.

Priscilla started straightening her makeup and hair, looking a little embarrassed. She quietly asked me to send them away.

"Thanks for the beer," I said, downing it and handing the cup back. "How about letting the lady get dressed?"

"Pardon us, we'll definitely do that," one of them said as they wobbled off, still blind drunk from the night before.

By mid-afternoon, we were bouncing down the Stanislaus in white-water rubber rafts. I kept an eye on Priscilla and told her to stick close to me in case we capsized. The rapids were dangerous and could suck you under, and you'd shoot right on, into rocks and tree stumps. Before the day was out, we were all black and blue from spills, even me; I'd spent a lot of time rescuing people.

When we returned to the camp, everyone was in awe of the jumbo Jeep and wanted to ride with me and Priscilla that night to the barbecue joint in town. On the way the cowboys grabbed the roll bar, and tried to rock the Jeep over. It held tight, defeating their best efforts.

After dinner, the bill was presented to Priscilla. Everyone looked to see if she would pick it up. She completely ignored the bill so they switched their attention to me, assuming I had to be loaded to be with her. Trapped, I picked up the tab for the whole table.

I knew that Priscilla was accustomed to Elvis's flamboyant life-style and that I would have to maintain his standards to keep her interested in me. When I got to know her better and she described what their actual life had been like, it was an eye-opener. I could have saved a lot of money. They stayed home, often for days at a time, hostages to each other, watching TV and sleeping behind closed doors and blackout curtains. Trays of Southern specialties—cornbread, mashed potatoes, meat loaf, pork chops, and banana pudding—were left outside their bedroom door by a beloved black cook, who'd knock and say, "Dinner's heah, Mister Evalis."

A black mammy had raised me in Pensacola, and I felt closer to Priscilla because of the similarities in our background. My mammy's name was Gussie, and she had a wooden leg that squeaked when she walked—a sound I came to love. Like Elvis's cook, she loved fixing Southern specialties.

Sunday morning we waved good-bye to the newlyweds and their guests, including the two cowboys who were actually realtors from San Francisco, now clean-shaven and neatly dressed.

I refilled the cooler with beer for our trip back to L.A. On the freeway, a big truck roared past. Priscilla grabbed my leg, shaking it excitedly.

Shouting over the wind, she said, "I love big semis. They're so powerful."

There was another one, further back, all red and chrome. I slowed the Jeep to seventy, letting the big rig pull up alongside us.

"Oh my God! It's so gorgeous!" she hollered.

"Look at our reflection in the hubcaps," I said. "You can see the whole Jeep reflected, with us in it."

We were so intrigued that we drove for miles in tandem with the truck, watching ourselves in the chrome hubcaps.

We were drinking beer, and Priscilla was waving and

screaming at the driver, "I love your truck!" He kept smiling and grinning back at her and motioning for us to pull over.

"I think he thinks you're saying, 'I love to fuck'!"

She stopped waving immediately. I stepped on the gas and barrel-assed back to Beverly Hills.

10

I wanted to impress Priscilla in every way, and one day
I took her to lunch at the Beverly Hills Hotel to meet my
aunt, Bonnie Silberstein, whose husband, Ben, owned the
hotel. We were shown to table number one in the Polo
Lounge, the prime spot, facing the entrance. Bonnie was
my father's sister, and she explained to Priscilla the bizarre
circumstances of how I was finally reunited with my father. From the time he'd left when I was six months old,
I'd never heard from him. I didn't know any of his side of
the family for years. Then one day Bonnie saw my Johnson's Baby Oil spread in *Seventeen*.

"I knew instantly you were an Edwards man," she said
proudly. "You had that full mouth and ruby lips."

Bonnie tracked me down through Nina Blanchard and
got my father and me together. Dad and I tried on numerous occasions to establish a relationship, but it never
worked out. We had nothing to say to each other. I knew
he felt guilty over not having had a part in raising his only

son. He must have had his reasons for not even so much as sending me a postcard, but it still puzzled me.

Priscilla and Bonnie hit it off marvelously, both being gracious ladies. When we finished eating, I noticed that Priscilla had begun to do something strange. Though we were seated with the queen of the hotel, and had half a dozen waiters hovering over us anticipating our every need, Priscilla was stacking her plates. After she finished with hers, she started in on mine, placing them in one big pile and shoving them to the side of the table.

Bonnie's eyes bulged, but she continued talking as if nothing had happened. When Priscilla started in on the silverware, I nudged her under the table to stop her.

"What did I do wrong?" she asked later. "You had such a strange look on your face."

"Baby, you don't have to clear tables," I explained.

"I always did it for Elvis. He didn't like dirty dishes in front of him, ever."

She was just a child-woman, I realized, still acting out the role Elvis had made her play for so many years. I was touched and wanted to protect her and keep her as innocent and adorable as she still was.

We'd only known each other for a few weeks, but I decided we had to live together. One night, coming out of the movies in Westwood, I said, "I care for you more than I have for anyone else. I want us to live together."

We stopped in at Maria's Italian restaurant for a bite of supper, and Priscilla said, "I don't know, Michael. I just broke up with someone. I wanted to enjoy my freedom for a while."

Her previous boyfriend had only recently cleared his belongings out of her house. All that was left of him was his cigarillos, and I'd noticed a few in the bedroom, still in an elegant little crystal glass.

We continued seeing each other day and night, and later on that summer, as August approached, Priscilla told me that Lisa would soon be leaving for summer camp. By now we did everything together, and on the morning Lisa was set to leave, I pulled the Jeep out into the driveway. Lisa, accompanied by a girlfriend, came slowly out of the house, moody and quiet. She wasn't happy about having to go to camp. When she saw me putting their bags in the Jeep, she perked up immediately.

"Are we going in that?" she asked. "I get to sit in front!"

Her friend was the daughter of one of Elvis's Memphis buddies, and Lisa shoved her in the back seat. And when Priscilla came out, Lisa got shoved in the back. And if Elvis had been able to come out, I'd have probably been shoved in the back, too. This was the first time I saw something about Lisa that I didn't like. She'd seen her dad ordering people around Graceland and was doing the same thing with her girlfriend. I wouldn't want my own daughter to be like that and wondered how I could help Lisa get rid of this arrogant attitude.

We were in the middle of a hot spell, and it was already in the nineties when we left the city that morning. About an hour later, driving through the burning desert, I spotted a state reservoir near the highway.

"I'm pulling off the road," I announced. "We're going swimming."

"Where?" the girls asked.

"In that lake over there."

"You're not allowed to swim in there," Priscilla said. "It's a reservoir." She drew my attention to a sign clearly stating that boating and fishing were permitted, but swimming was strictly prohibited.

"Priscilla," I said, "boats are allowed, with all their gas and oil—but you can't swim? Come on, we're going in."

We all leapt out of the Jeep and ran to the reservoir, Priscilla leading the way. Soon we were all splashing around, the girls in their underwear and me skinny-dipping. I dove under the water and came up under Priscilla, pinching her foot. She screamed in terror, and I bobbed to the surface, yelling, "It's the creature from the black lagoon!" I swam after the girls, going "Aaaaaarrrrrrrgh! I'm going to get you!" They squealed with delight and paddled away as fast as they could.

I yelled for Priscilla to watch me and, floating up onto my back, I created a human fountain. The girls didn't know whether to giggle or gasp, and Priscilla was so shocked by my display that she choked on some water.

"Michael, don't!" she scolded. "You shouldn't do that."

"It's all my years of living in Europe," I said, laughing. "People over there are a lot less uptight about things like taking a leak. Everybody is always stopping along the highway and doing it right there in broad daylight, and no one thinks a thing about it."

"But in front of children?"

"My God, woman! They pee, too."

But she had a point. I wasn't in Europe anymore.

Still, these were my women now, and I wanted them to live the way I did—fun-filled and daring.

"Forget that whole uptight world," I said. "It'll make you grow old too fast. Let's you and me and Lisa do things our way."

11

Priscilla became a different woman with me when Lisa was away. Free from the responsibilities of motherhood, she even got a little risqué. That was the side of her I liked best. With Lisa off at camp, though I still hadn't moved into her house, Priscilla and I made love endlessly—in the pool, then while showering afterward, then on the chaise, in the kitchen, and even in the maid's quarters, my favorite place. In the maid's room we'd fantasize Priscilla was the maid and I was the master, seducing her. She'd put on a French accent and make up dialogue to turn me on.

"Oh, monsieur, stop! What are you doing? Hurry! Madame might catch us!"

"Do as I say or I will have to spank you!"

I craved Priscilla constantly and was driven in my desire that we live together. One night, crawling into Priscilla's bed, I said, "All I use my place for anymore is to change clothes."

Teasing, I added, "And also to pick up all the messages from all the girls wondering where I've disappeared to."

Taking her into my arms, coaxing her, I said, "And I'd rather be spending all that rent money buying perfume for you."

"Why can't we keep things the way they are?" she asked. "We're happy, we're having fun together. Why change anything?"

I had to smile. This was a girl who'd been cooped up in a celebrity mausoleum since she was fourteen years old. And then all of a sudden I'd come into her life—a gypsy spirit encouraging her to break free, spread her wings, and fly with the wind. I couldn't blame her for not wanting me to move in.

"All I'm saying is I don't like being away from you," I told her.

"I don't like being away from you, either, Michael. But I think having your own place is good."

"I'd still have my own place," I said.

"What do you mean?"

"I could always sleep in my Jeep if we needed time apart."

I looked at her soulfully, and she broke up.

"I love you, baby," I said. "Don't you miss me when I'm not with you?"

"Yes," she nodded.

"We could have something very special."

"Let me think about it."

"What's there to think about?"

I told her that at the end of the week I had to go to New York and that I was going to be working with a lot of beautiful models—and I didn't want anything to jeopardize us. If we moved in together, I'd know we were definitely committed to each other and I'd want to be faithful. The following day she consented to help me move from my high-rise apartment in Hollywood to her home in Beverly Hills.

We waited until late at night to begin the move, because she was afraid someone might see us.

"Relax. We're not characters in some spy novel," I said naively. I still had no idea what it was to be associated with the Presley name, but I was about to find out.

"You don't know how clever they are," she said, referring to the paparazzi and the tabloids. Indeed they were. A gossip columnist who lived in my building reported our every move that night as Priscilla and I sneaked in and out of the apartment, carrying my things to the Jeep parked in the garage.

After gathering up my clothes, I looked around at the rest of my belongings and decided I didn't want to keep any of them. They reminded me too much of Maggie and Ron. Priscilla was astounded I didn't want to keep anything, but, close as we'd become, I couldn't tell her my reason.

"You can't throw everything away," she protested.

She went into the bedroom and examined the bed.

"Let's take the mattress," she suggested, "and your sheets —they're better than mine."

"They're really old," I lied, still thinking of Maggie.

"Michael, don't be silly," Priscilla persisted. "They're practically brand new!"

"Take whatever you want," I finally said, finding it impossible to explain my reasons without hurting her.

Moving into the kitchen, she noticed my professional cookware hanging over the stove.

"I didn't know you cooked," she said, impressed.

"You've never experienced *haute cuisine* until you've tried mine! There'll be drinking and dancing naked and all kinds of unique appetizers before the main course . . . me. No, I'm just kidding."

She looked intrigued and said, "Well, for sure we'll take the pots and pans."

I followed her into the living room, where she examined the elegant glass-topped desk and chrome and black-leather chairs.

"These are very expensive," she observed, "but they don't look like your taste."

She was right. Ron had loaned them to me and later told me to keep them.

"They're rented," I said. The last thing I wanted was to have anything of Ron's in Priscilla's house. And as I closed the door to my apartment I realized I was opening the door on a new life.

The next morning, in my new home in Beverly Hills, I unpacked my clothes and hung them up in my bathroom. It was so huge that it included a dressing room, furnished with an antique stove that had been converted into a sink, and a suede-upholstered barber's chair. It was three times the size of the first apartment I'd had in New York.

We had the whole house to ourselves, and though I was fond of Lisa, I was glad she was away at camp—and that the servants were on vacation.

To celebrate my moving in, I decided to surprise Priscilla by cooking her an elaborate dinner. I started preparing a whole fish Barcelona style, and Priscilla exclaimed, "Aren't you going to cut the head off?"

"No, all its juice would leak out."

Holding up the fish and wiggling it at her, I said, "We wouldn't want that, would we?"

She blushed and said, "Michael, you're terrible."

"It's true," I said. "All the best juices are in its head."

I taught her how to cook the fish—de-vein six large shrimp and stuff them inside; chop up a whole garlic, tomato, onion, and potatoes, and add these around the fish in a casserole. Pour olive oil lightly all over and then empty your wine glass into it. Take every herb in your spice cabinet, pour some of each in the palm of your hand, and, rubbing your hands together vigorously, let it rain on the fish. Never sprinkle herbs direct from the container; they have to be ground in your hand to bring out the full bouquet. Cover and bake at 375 degrees. By the time you finish having a quickie, about forty-five minutes later, the fish will be ready to eat—and so will you.

We enjoyed our candlelight dinner down by the pool. It was our nuptial feast, and we both had a lot to drink, celebrating the big decision we'd made. Working on our third bottle of wine, Priscilla got very excited as she told me about a telephone game she liked to play.

"Here, I'll show you," she said, grabbing the phone. She punched out seven numbers at random, and when someone answered, she lowered her voice to a sultry whisper.

"Hi, big boy. Have you missed me? I've sure missed you."

It was wonderful watching her impersonate a hooker.

"Oh, don't act that way," she continued. "You know who this is. You know what I want. Oh, you're being so naughty. I like that."

Suddenly she cracked up laughing, couldn't stop, and had to hang up.

She wanted to play a variation of the game on Joanie Esposito Kardashian, ex-wife of Elvis's road manager, Joe

Esposito. Priscilla got as far as dialing Joanie, but the line was busy. That didn't deter her for a minute, and she resumed her game of random dialing. Something about it touched a place in my heart, and I felt the first stirrings of love for her that evening.

12

The first time I was struck senseless by love was in high school. I can still recall that night—my sweetheart Betty Lynn and I were alone in the dark, in the back seat of my Chevy, and I fell in love. The next evening at the supper table, my throat got so tight I couldn't swallow. I was hungry but couldn't eat and I pushed my untouched plate of food away. No one ever forgets the first time of falling victim to love sickness, that sudden gnawing sensation that starts at the very bottom of your gut and slowly works its way up until it has your entire insides in its grip. You can't think straight, eat, or do almost anything but pine for your sweetheart.

I had the same obsession now for Priscilla, I realized, as I came to the end of my shooting in New York. Those bittersweet symptoms had me in their grip once more, and I couldn't think of anything but holding Priscilla in my arms again. I rushed back to my hotel each night after work, looking forward to hearing her voice on long distance. Finally we decided she should come to New York and join me when my work was completed.

For the last three days I'd been modeling Italian suits, working with two girls as my partners. One was a dark-haired Dutch model, and the other was a freckle-faced Texan. We were shooting in an unusual location—the dilapidated, rotting piers along Manhattan's West Side. The European designer wanted a daring contast for his sleek-looking clothes, a stark background that would really make them stand out. Accommodating his wishes, the photographer chose the pier for its run-down warehouses and sleazy look and told us to be sexy in the photos. In situations like this, when models are expected to turn each other on, you more than likely end up having an affair. But now I had Priscilla Presley on my mind, and she and the legend she stood for blocked out all desire for other women. I felt relieved to be off the fast track for the first time since I couldn't remember when. When she arrived in New York we flew into each others arms like lovers who'd been separated for a decade instead of a few days.

A photographer friend of mine, Bill Conners, invited us to stay with him in his East Side brownstone. Going down the hall to the bedroom, our hands were all over each other. We didn't even make it as far as the bedroom, ducking into the first bathroom we came to. Priscilla surprised me with her aggressiveness and had her way with me. As I looked down at her, I thought to myself, I finally have all I've searched for in a woman.

That first evening we all went dancing at Studio 54, where I introduced Priscilla to *sambucca*, a 100-proof aperitif that you drink with roasted coffee beans in it. We toasted each other the whole night through, eating all the coffee beans and getting smashed. Back home, in the garden at four o'clock in the morning, I held Priscilla's forehead as she threw up in Bill's petunias and gladioli.

"I remember holding my mother's head like this one time when she was sick," I told her.

"You must be very close," she said as we went back inside.

"You're very much like her. You're both so feminine."

The following day, aimlessly window-shopping along Fifth Avenue, nursing our hangovers, we paused at a newsstand and saw a headline about Elvis. The photo accompanying the story showed him at his worst, all puffed and bloated. I feared sad memories might ruin Priscilla's weekend and, hoping to take her mind off him, I took her to my favorite sushi restaurant, Miyakawa.

"We can have some hot sake," I said. "It's the best remedy for our heads. You know, hair of the dog."

"I'm sorry," she said after we took our shoes off and settled down in a private room. "He died exactly a year ago today . . . August 16, 1977."

The sake only made her feel worse. On our way home, I began to feel terrible for her. Stopping on Fifth Avenue between Forty-ninth and Fiftieth, in the midst of the rushing crowd, I felt a desperate urge to hold her. She cuddled up to me and after a moment I opened my eyes and saw the facade of Saint Patrick's Cathedral rising majestically in front of us.

"Look, Priscilla," I said, and gently turned her.

"Could we go inside?" she asked. "I'd like to very much."

We entered the cool, hushed serenity of the cathedral, and it was like coming upon a clearing in a forest, still and timeless. We knelt in a pew and bowed our heads. I asked

God to ease her mind, and to help her overcome whatever confusion she might be feeling about Elvis.

Before we left, she said she wanted to light a candle. I followed her to the long row of candles by the door, and I lit one, too.

"What did you pray for?" I asked as we left Saint Patrick's, stepping out into the afternoon brightness.

"I can't tell you that. I just hope he's happy and peaceful."

The experience in the church comforted her, but it was disturbing to me. I prayed to God to make Priscilla mine and help her through her pain and grief. I also prayed that I wouldn't be just another heartache for her and Lisa. They'd had enough already. The last time I'd prayed was sixteen years earlier in marine boot camp when the drill instructor had tried to break my spirit with severe punishment. We walked up Fifth Avenue toward Central Park, and sat for a while under the cool trees. Surrounded by trees and green grass and happy children, our spirits were lifted.

To further cheer us up I suggested that we accept Bill's invitation to visit him at his beach house on Fire Island, in a gay community known as the Pines.

We made the short flight in a seaplane, taking off from the East River near the Brooklyn Bridge. Suddenly this woman who had commanded her own private jet became enthralled as the tiny seaplane flew us over the Great South Bay to the Pines. Wearing tight-fitting jeans, T-shirt, thin-strapped sandles, with her hair in braids, she looked like the same little princess that Elvis had spotted back in Weisbaden almost twenty years earlier.

When the seaplane landed in the bay, Priscilla saw some

passengers wading out toward us for the return flight to Manhattan.

"That looks like fun," she said.

When we stepped from the pontoons into the bay, I swept her up and started to carry her.

She struggled to get down, saying, "I want to run through the water!"

We loaded our luggage in a little red wagon tethered to the dock, with Bill's name painted on it. There were no cars, only boardwalks, so we proceeded on foot to Bill's beach house. After unpacking, we started back to the harbor.

"If we hurry," I explained, "we can just make Tea Dance."

"Tea Dance?" she said. "What's that?"

"Just wait and see. It's going to blow your mind."

On the boardwalk, we passed a well-known cruising spot.

"That's the meat rack," I said. "It's slang for the bushes, and guys meet there for casual sex."

Priscilla said, "What if someone's a vegetarian?"

"Believe me, out here there's something for everyone—and more."

In the distance we could see the crowd on the sun deck at the Boatel and feel the vibrations from the disco's powerful speakers. Laughing male couples hurried past us, their arms around each other. Tea Dance was in full swing. Someone called to me from the crowd, and I spotted Bill, who leaned over the railing to help us up. Suddenly we were standing in the midst of hundreds of dripping-wet, bare-chested guys, each body better-looking than the next, faces suntanned, hair slicked, and everyone embracing, drinking, and chattering. Priscilla's eyes were as big as saucers.

"I've never seen so many beautiful men in all my life. Are you sure they're all gay?"

I went to get our drinks, and when I came back Bill and two friends with rippling stomach muscles surrounded Priscilla. She was laughing and sipping a kamikaze someone had handed her. I was impressed that Priscilla could make herself at home so quickly in such a far-out crowd.

After Tea Dance, we went back to Bill's house for a big, informal dinner, rested awhile, and then went out dancing all night at the Sandpiper, a disco in the harbor.

We slept late, like everyone else in the Pines. Waking at noon I wrapped my arms around her drowsy body and pulled her to me. I kissed the back of her neck and slid my hand between her thighs, feeling the special warmth that is always there when a woman first wakes.

Reaching down to the floor, I found the wine bottle from the night before and took a big swig for myself and another for Priscilla, giving it to her from my lips. I swung around and started massaging her feet. Noticing she was uncomfortable in the harsh sunlight flooding the room, I reached up above my head and drew the shades. As I slid back down in the bed, I started softly massaging her with my toes. It was an incredible turn-on.

I wanted to be her demon lover and, gently spreading her legs, made love to her.

I always felt a need to come up with things that Elvis might not have done with her, and often during our relationship I found myself searching for new thrills for us to experience.

That afternoon we decided to go clamming. Standing

waist-deep in the bay, I taught her the best way to dig for clams.

"Pretend you're doing the Twist," I explained.

I could feel clams underfoot immediately, but Priscilla wasn't having any luck.

"I'm no good at this," she said.

I reassured her, and in a moment she let out a squeal, saying, "I've found one!" But when she reached down, she unknowingly pulled up a mud-covered rock.

"That's a really big one!" I said, pretending it was a clam. I didn't want her to give up, so I grabbed the rock and dropped it in the bucket with the clams. "You're a natural-born clammer," I praised. When she wasn't looking, I threw it away.

Her confidence restored, we managed to fill up the bucket in an hour. Later, while the clams lay soaking under the hose on the sundeck, we polished off a bottle of Montrachet. Using my Nikon, we began taking nude pictures.

Alone in the house, we wrapped ourselves in towels and I prepared the linguini and clams the way I'd learned in Italy. Then we sat down to a tasty dinner and continued taking sexy pictures.

"I don't know how you do it," she said. "You can make the simplest things interesting."

I understood what she was trying to tell me. She was starving for adventure, and I was giving it to her nonstop —dancing till dawn, sleeping under the stars, shooting the rapids, revels in exotic resorts, eating in the nude, and exploring our sexuality.

"I'm not afraid to experience anything with you, Michael," she said.

I wanted to take her in my arms, to say I love you and

ask her to marry me, but I couldn't. I knew it was too soon, and I didn't want to scare her away.

She glanced over at the fireplace and asked me to build a fire. She wanted to sit and talk for a while. When I got a fire going, she curled up beside me, smoothing my hair as we gazed into the flames.

"We hardly know each other," she said, "and we're already living together."

I knew this would have been the perfect moment to express our feelings for each other and to go deeper emotionally, but I simply didn't know how. To hide my insecurity, I took her in my arms. Our lovemaking that night left us lying breathless. Later, when Priscilla looked up at me, I saw a sadness in her eyes, and I didn't know why. It bothered me, and I realized that if I wanted to win this woman's love, it was going to take more than just satisfying her in bed.

I decided to take her home to meet my family.

13

When I was growing up, Mother called me her Little Man. I was raised with love generously given by my mammy Gussie, my grandmother, and Mom, who was gentle and sensitive and had to be both mother and father to me. Mom painstakingly taught me not only all the social graces but also to be a man of character. I looked forward to sharing Mom with Priscilla. I also wanted Priscilla to know that I was a stable father to Caroline, and even during my European years had managed to hold the family together with postcards, money, and long-distance love. She would see another whole side of me once we got home. So far she'd only experienced my carefree, adventurous nature, and I wanted to open her eyes to the fact there was more to me than just someone to have fun with.

When I was a kid Mom had always told me that it was up to me to protect and take care of my sister and her. Though being deserted by Dad made me feel unwanted, I swore I'd become everything he never was, and one day I'd find a way to make Mother and Jeannie proud of me. So there was a special significance for me in bringing Priscilla to Pensacola to meet Mother. It fulfilled my childhood promise. I was a small-town boy bringing home his famous girl.

We took a train from New York to New Orleans. Booking the best sleeping compartment available, I loaded up with Dom Perignon for the long trip. I can still remember the look of disbelief on the conductor's face when he discovered we were going all the way to New Orleans.

"Do you folks realize you're on a milk train?"

We hadn't, but soon did, when it started stopping in every small town between New York and Louisiana. We enjoyed ourselves anyway, writing poetry to one another, sipping champagne, and trying to find a workable way to make love in the small bunk beds.

The conductor's cry of "New Orleans, next stop!" was one of the most welcome sounds we'd ever heard. You never saw two people hop off a train faster. We stayed at Maison de Ville, a little hotel tucked away in an alley in the French Quarter. Dining at Brennan's, we guzzled gin fizzes and feasted on oysters Rockefeller. After listening to Sweet Emma and her jazz band at Preservation Hall, we hit a strip joint in the Quarter. In the bar, a transvestite latched on to Priscilla, introducing herself as Robert and insisting on buying us a round of drinks. Her voice rising from base to falsetto, she asked us to call her Rochelle. She was still learning how to talk like a woman, she explained as her voice kept slipping.

As we left, Rochelle followed us out into the squalid, early morning streets. Walking back to the hotel, Rochelle let all the street people know that she was with Priscilla Presley and made grand introductions left and right, oblivious to their who-gives-a-shit responses.

We said good-bye to her in front of our hotel.

"I'd always wanted to meet you, Priscilla," she said. "Your husband changed my life! I'd always wanted a sex change, and seeing how he wasn't afraid of expressing himself—it gave me the courage to become the real me."

The next day, driving down to Point Clear, Alabama, we checked into the Grand Hotel. I'd dreamed of staying there ever since I'd visited the hotel with my grandparents when I was a kid. Grandpa liked to walk around the grounds pretending he was a big shot, but the hotel was expensive and we couldn't afford to spend the night.

Priscilla and I found it insufferably stuffy and checked out the next morning. It wasn't what I'd remembered as a child, but somehow, staying the night, I felt I'd done it for Grandpa.

The only thing we liked there was an old black dog we found wandering around the grounds. We made friends with him, and Priscilla persuaded me to go into the kitchen and get some scraps for him. Later we wrote a poem about his big paws that he planted on our chests as he stretched and yawned.

When we reached Pensacola, before taking Priscilla to my mother's I drove by the house I was raised in, and she said it reminded her of Elvis's birthplace in Tupelo, Mississippi. It was a little white frame house with a low, cracked, red-brick wall that Grandpa and I had built. It had a chimney and a latticed porch covered with morning glories. Priscilla said it was charming.

When we reached Mom's, my daughter came running out to meet us in the driveway. At eleven and a half years old, Caroline was very sensitive about the thick glasses she had to wear because of her astigmatism, and she never looked anyone in the eye. She was bashful and intimidated with Priscilla.

The first words she blurted in her nervousness were, "I know how to catch fish and can bait my own hook!" I had called her from New Orleans and told her that I'd take us all fishing out in the Gulf.

"Your daddy has told me a lot about you, Caroline," Priscilla said. "But you're much prettier than I could ever have imagined!"

Caroline beamed, flattered by Priscilla's words.

Mom joined us, excited and eager to welcome Priscilla into her home. "I'm so glad you came!" she said, putting her arms around Priscilla. "My son hasn't stopped saying nice things about you."

Priscilla whispered to me, "Your mom's great! Is she always this enthusiastic?"

"Always," I said.

Mother invited us inside, saying she'd saved a bottle of champagne just for a special occasion such as this. Then she brought out her camera. Mom loved to record every moment of family get-togethers.

"Would you mind if I took a picture?" she asked.

"Not now, Mom. We just got here."

"No, let her, Michael," Priscilla said. "My dad's the same way. I'd like you to meet my parents, Mrs. Edwards."

"I'd love to, but please call me Charlotte."

Priscilla had been clinging to me during this entire exchange. She looked up at me, her eyes shining.

Sitting in the living room later with my whole family around me, Caroline at my feet, Priscilla under one arm and Mom under the other, I was surrounded with love. It reminded me of the time at Magic Mountain with Priscilla,

Lisa and her friend. I hoped I wouldn't ever lose this feeling.

The next afternoon I took Caroline and Priscilla fishing, as I'd promised. I hired a boat and crew, and it took us several hours to reach the Gulf Stream, where the big-game fishing is good. We were about twenty-five miles out, and by midnight Priscilla and I were well into a bottle of rum and starving for the delicious-smelling steaks the captain was barbecuing for dinner.

"It sure is dark out here," I said. "Not a star in the sky."

"It's as if we're the only people left in the world," she said. "I haven't seen another boat all night."

"Think of all the creatures swimming below us."

"Michael, you'll scare Caroline."

As the smoke grew thicker from the sizzling steaks, I began to feel queasy. In a little while, I noticed Priscilla had gotten awfully quiet herself.

"Daddy, I'm sick," Caroline said. I called out to Priscilla to help, but she was leaning over the railing, trying to keep me from seeing her throw up. When she finished she turned to me, and daintily dabbed at the corner of her mouth. I was astounded that anyone could throw up without making a single gagging noise, but, as I gradually came to understand, she would rather die than be embarrassed.

Needing desperately to lie down, Priscilla and Caroline made their way below, into the darkness of the cabin, holding onto each other for support. I told the captain that the ladies were sick and we had to head back.

I went below with a bunch of ice cubes in a towel. Caroline was lying on a bunk in the dimly lit cabin with Priscilla holding her forehead. Though she was fighting her own nausea, Priscilla was bravely carrying on and doing her best to help my daughter. As soon as Caroline fell asleep, I helped Priscilla into the adjoining bunk. Then I knelt beside her and we gazed at each other for a long time.

"When I look into your eyes I feel like a child again," she said. "I'm no longer afraid to let my feelings show. All of my fears and pain are still there, but this time I don't want to hide them."

She was the first woman who'd ever told me anything that deeply personal about herself.

"I've never allowed anyone to get this close before, Michael. I trust you more than anyone I've ever been involved with."

When we left Pensacola, Priscilla insisted that Mom come to Beverly Hills for a long visit. Priscilla later told me, "I've never felt such warmth from anyone. Your mother is wonderful." She also invited Caroline, who promised to visit us soon.

When we returned to Beverly Hills, we weren't the same two people who'd left two weeks earlier. There was now such a bond between us that we couldn't bear to be separated from one another. But we had to be, because my work involved a lot of travel, and it was not always possible to bring Priscilla along. I explained to her that a film crew is a tightly knit little family, and outsiders never quite fit in. They always feel left out.

"I know what you mean," she said. "I noticed that when I visited Elvis on the set."

But she still wasn't happy about my frequent absences. Unfortunately I made the mistake of telling Priscilla about my past affairs with the models I'd worked with around the world; I said that when a bunch of attractive models are thrown together on location, in strange and lonely places, falling into bed together is virtually inevitable. It seemed to come from not having anything to hold onto, but now that Priscilla was in my life, I felt all that changing.

Shortly after our return from New York I had to fly to Acapulco to shoot *Glamour*, then to Seattle for Nordstrum's. Catching the red-eye to New York, I had back-to-back bookings for Macy's, *Woman's Day*, *Modern Bride*, and *Vogue Patterns*. No sooner was I home than Wrangler jeans brought me to Denver. From Colorado I had to fly directly to Monterey for a Revlon shooting in Carmel. I called Priscilla from the Ventana Inn, inviting her to come up and join me, but then the agency phoned and said I had to come back to L.A. the following morning for a Japanese golf apparel commercial. The Japanese were amusing to work with, always making me face the sun so I'd squint and look Oriental. But the real bread and butter of modeling, besides a big ad campaign, was catalog work. When I was in L.A., I worked regularly in the huge photo studios of May Co., Robinson's, and the Broadway. Every morning at the breakfast table, Priscilla and Lisa proudly showed me my full-page ads in the *Los Angeles Times*.

From the night I met Priscilla, I continually urged her to pursue her own interests and to carve out a career of her own. I set up a shooting for her with a photographer friend of mine from New York, Peter Vaeth. When Peter sent us the enlargements, I was very impressed. He'd photographed her in the back of an old pickup truck, with her hair up and looking very seductive with her hands pressed together between her legs. He also captured a very lusty side of her in jeans. This was the first time Priscilla had worked with a top-flight New York fashion photographer, and I could already see the wheels beginning to turn in her head.

"You really should get into modeling right away," I told her.

"Do you think I could do commercials?"

"Sexy and beautiful as you are, you could do anything you wanted—mascara, lipstick, shampoo, anything."

I was constantly amazed that this incredible-looking woman had such doubts about her looks, but eventually she hired a manager and dived into her career. Though she disliked giving up her privacy, she agreed to numerous interviews her manager arranged with producers, directors, and studio executives. It took up so much of her time that I found myself looking after her eleven-year-old daughter in her absence. I had fun playing papa to Lisa and supportive mate to Priscilla.

After summer camp, Lisa had gone to Memphis to stay at Graceland. Once there, as usual, she didn't want to leave. Right after Labor Day Priscilla called her and said, "Come on home, Yittle One. It's time to get ready for the new school year."

"No," Lisa argued. "I don't want to come back yet."

Lisa wasn't happy in Beverly Hills, where she had few friends. At Graceland everyone doted on her, Elvis's family, friends, and staff. She had the run of the place and really took over, ordering everyone around just like a miniature Elvis. She loved Elvis's cousin Patsy and liked to spend hours talking with her, lying in bed and watching the soaps and playing cards.

Finally Priscilla had to put her foot down. She demanded that Lisa return to L.A. at once. When she got home, they continued to argue like two feuding schoolgirls. Stubborn and strong-willed even at eleven, Lisa behaved like her father in many ways. She kept her door closed and her blackout curtains drawn. When I told Lisa, "I don't think all that darkness is good for you," she ignored me. It was a long time before Lisa allowed me to get close to her. In the beginning, when I'd looked like just another boyfriend of Priscilla's things had been okay. But now that I was obviously something more serious, Lisa wanted it known that no one was going to take the place of her father. She made this clear by keeping a cool distance.

I went to Priscilla and asked her how I should deal with Lisa. She told me Lisa was a very private person and to be patient and wait. "Lisa will come to you when she's ready. Try not to take it personally. That's just the way she is." I followed Priscilla's advice and left Lisa alone.

Neither Priscilla nor I had had what you would call a stable upbringing, and we were now having to invent our roles as we went along. Creating stability behind the big black gates wasn't easy, especially trying to fill Elvis's place in Lisa's life when she didn't want it. But Priscilla was right—by not forcing the issue, eventually I managed to get Lisa to come to me on her own. I played her game. Soon my patience was rewarded, and Lisa gradually warmed up to me. But I still wondered if I possessed the understanding and maturity to make this a happy family.

14

It was winter in L.A., which meant cold nights and clear, star-filled skies, with Santa Ana winds frequently blowing warm gusts of air in from the desert. Arriving home late one evening, after an all-day shooting, as I climbed out of my Jeep I was engulfed by an unusually strong Santa Ana condition. I loved this time of year in Southern California, although you couldn't be certain whether it was winter or summer. To me, nothing was ever boring about L.A., even the weather.

The house was empty, but Priscilla had left a note telling me that she and Lisa had gone over to her parents for dinner and to join them there. I was tired and decided to stay home and relax, so I grabbed a Heineken from the refrigerator and went into the den. Flipping the stereo to KACE, the soft jazz station, I settled on the sofa, guzzled half my beer, laid my head back, and closed my eyes. We'd now been living together a little more than a year. I savored moments like this, having the house to myself. In the quiet, I often thought about Elvis. Not Elvis the superstar, but

Elvis the father and husband. I could imagine him sitting over there with Lisa at the lime-green piano, puffing his wooden-tipped cigar, flicking ashes on the carpet, laughing as Priscilla scolded him for being so sloppy, and blowing smoke rings at her.

I opened my eyes, realizing it was now me that Elvis's Lisa was coming to for hugs, and the realization was gratifying. I finished my beer and bent the can in half, then got up and walked down the hall, past our bedroom, toward Lisa's room, the most secluded part of the house, where an entire section of the wall was lined with family photographs. They were carefully framed in Lucite boxes with red trim, and it gave me a warm feeling, examining this intimate record of Elvis's life. I especially liked to look at the photos of Elvis with Lisa. Their embraces were so tender and I could see so much love that it made me want to cry out in sorrow for them. Why did he have to be taken away from her, leaving a legacy that neither she nor Priscilla was capable of coping with alone?

"I want to know about you, Michael," Priscilla had said. "What your fears are . . . your dreams. A woman has to know those things about her man. It makes her feel like she's needed. We talk a lot, but you don't really tell me what you're thinking. You keep it all so tightly protected inside that I feel left out sometimes. It's what I loved about Elvis. He was so sensitive and he wasn't afraid to share that with me."

I told her I didn't mean to hide anything, I just found it hard talking about certain feelings. I was afraid I wouldn't like what I discovered about myself and usually tended to ignore feelings of weakness. She told me that sharing those things was the only way we could grow together. I replied that what you said about yourself wasn't nearly as important as your actions. Still I realized that if I ever hoped for happiness with Priscilla, she was right, I'd have to give all of me—and be willing to undertake that search of the heart.

I returned the picture of Elvis and Lisa to its hook on the wall, and went to our bedroom. Priscilla's bathroom door was ajar, and I went inside and slid open one of the mirrored doors. I knew Priscilla kept Elvis's army jacket in the closet, and, for some reason I wanted to look at it. I took it off the hanger and examined it. It was soft and faded from many washings and had Presley stenciled over the right breast pocket. I could tell it was my size and I thought about putting it on, but I didn't. This jacket was very special to her, a reminder of their simpler, happier days together in Germany. She trusted me so completely with all of his things around the house that I felt it would be wrong. I hung it up and returned to the kitchen for another beer. Priscilla had told me that Elvis had never been the same after the army, and I understood why. When I'd first come home on leave after boot camp, Mother had told me it was the only time in her life she'd ever been afraid of me —I acted so rigid about everything and every other word out of my mouth was "fuck." She felt that the marines had destroyed the gentler side of my nature, the quality she loved best in me. She was partly right; it did bring out the harsher side of me, and I'm sure it had done the same thing to Elvis. But though it changed both of us I believed the change was only on the surface, rather than inside. If Elvis was like me, and I believed he was, in his heart he still had gentleness.

I would have been a good buddy for Elvis. He needed someone like me around him, who liked to be outdoors, swimming, jogging, camping out, roughing it. He'd have loved my big Jeep, too, and I'm sure the instant he saw it he'd have junked his sissy little golf cart. The two of us could have headed for the hills and maybe even chased a woman or two. All he really needed was a strong male companion for him to believe in.

I'd recently told Lisa how much I loved her dad when I was her age, and that I grew up with his music and developed my own independence from watching him. She looked at me, not replying.

"You ever think about singing?"

"Not really. I don't think Mommy would let me."

"I'm sure she would if you told her you wanted to."

She just shrugged her shoulders, but I persisted. "I know you have a pretty voice," I said. "I've heard you in your room."

"I took piano lessons once."

"Did you like it? Why don't you continue?"

I was trying to get Lisa enthusiastic about something, anything. She reminded me so much of myself when I was a kid, aloof, holding everything inside. I thought getting her interested in piano or voice would help her be less withdrawn and able to express some of that pent-up emotion and energy; I also had been unable to express it as a kid, always afraid that someone might laugh at me or tease me.

"It would have pleased your dad, I bet."

Lisa abruptly changed the subject, going over to a big wooden bowl of fruit on the kitchen table, selecting a mango, and bringing it over to me.

"Cut this up for me, like you do."

"If you say please."

"Please."

I dropped the subject for the time being and sliced the mango for her, using the technique I'd learned from islanders down in Barbados when I'd been there on location once. They taught me to slice the mango in half, remove the seed, cut crisscrosses in each half, then flip them up from underneath, which makes little bite-sized squares pop up, and you can then eat the mango without getting it stuck in your teeth. Lisa watched me in amazement as I prepared it, and she told me, "Don't forget to squeeze the lime on it. Please."

Among other reasons Elvis chose Priscilla over all the other girls was that she was young and didn't know the ropes; with her, his insecurities and fragile ego were completely safe. She was his protection, and he was hers—or so he thought. And then, unexpectedly, Lisa came along. They were suddenly faced with the reality of their situation and could no longer hide behind childish games. Abortion was considered, briefly, but Elvis's instinct for survival told him that the time had come for him to have a little Elvis. He needed something secure to hold onto now that his topsy-turvy marriage was beginning to fail him, and so was his career. Elvis had been right; shortly after Lisa's birth, his career took a spectacular upswing. But ironically his marriage didn't, and Priscilla ended up in the arms of another man. As I waited for my girls to return, I told myself I wouldn't make the same mistakes Elvis had.

I wanted Lisa to meet my daughter and invited Caroline to visit us in L.A. The two of them became fast friends immediately, Caroline sleeping in Lisa's room on the pullout bed. They stayed up half the night talking, sharing stories about their home, family, and boyfriends. They had so much in common, including the fact that they both had older boyfriends. Unknown to Priscilla and me, Lisa already had a boyfriend in Memphis, and Caroline had one in Pensacola. When I talked to my daughter years later, she told me that she and Lisa, like typical adolescents, had talked about nothing but boys and kissing and "doing it."

"Neither one of us had done it yet," Caroline said, "but we were both really interested in sharing what we knew about it."

That first morning, when they got up, they decided to go skinny-dipping. Neither of them had ever been swimming nude before.

"The funny part of it," Caroline later told me, "was we hardly knew each other. We teased each other, saying, 'You go in first.' 'No, you go.' Finally we decided to go together. We laughed and took pictures of each other naked, and kept on talking about boys and sex and doing it."

During the whole visit, the only argument the girls had was who got to sit in the front seat of the Jeep with me when I took them places. I loved the feeling but realized how sad the situation was. I was raising another man's daughter while my own daughter, fatherless, was thousands of miles away.

After a few weeks, Caroline began to miss her mom and told me she was ready to go home. She and Lisa made elaborate plans to keep in touch by telephone, and I kissed her and put her on a plane for Florida.

15

During our first year together, we became a hot item in the press. Everything they wrote about us was true. I enjoyed all the attention, happy for the world to know about our romance. But when the paparazzi wouldn't leave us alone, and I'd have to sneak Priscilla in and out of restaurants or nightclubs to keep them from mobbing us, I began to understand why Elvis lived behind blackout curtains and locked gates.

We went out every night, dancing until we practically dropped from exhaustion, and we came home at two or three o'clock, soaked to the skin. We were so caught up with each other that we were neglecting Lisa, Caroline, and everyone and everything else. With Lisa we attempted to make up for our absences by having breakfast together every morning and taking her out to dinner. It was hard on us because Lisa always wanted to go to McDonald's, and we wanted her to eat better food and experience fine dining.

"I don't like to sit in some dumb restaurant for hours,"

Lisa grumbled, "listening to you guys talk all the time. It's boring, boring, boring."

"I think you should learn about good restaurants for when you begin dating, Lisa," I pointed out.

"Whoever I date's going to take me to McDonald's or I'm not going out with him," Lisa said.

The press managed to track me down at Priscilla's home in Beverly Hills. Calling me on our unlisted phone, a reporter from *The Midnight Globe* begged and pleaded for an interview on me and my modeling career. I was thrilled, naively believing that he was genuinely interested in me and not just my relationship with Priscilla, and enthusiastically agreed to answer his questions. Later, when I mentioned the interview to Priscilla, she turned white.

"You didn't say anything, did you?" she asked.

"He asked me how I became a model," I said. "And I told him."

"Is that all?"

"Yes, except for one or two things, like how we met and if I'd taught you how to dance. He was very polite."

"Don't trust them, ever. They're cunning."

"I can read people, baby. You're being too suspicious."

"Wait and see," she said, obviously quite upset.

Shortly thereafter, *The Globe* broke a story headlined "Pris Presley's Disco-Beat Beau," with accompanying paparazzi shots showing us in each other's arms on the dance floor of an L.A. nightclub.

The world press followed with a barrage of stories detailing our every move. *The London Daily Express* headlined "Priscilla Puts Michael Under Her Spell," and wrote:

"That old Presley magic is at work again . . . the former wife of 'the King' has striking male model bewitched."

TV & Movie Screen headlined "Priscilla Presley's Life

with Her Live-in Lover," running a picture of us captioned, "She's the picture of happiness with new love." In the next column was a somber picture of her and Elvis with the caption: "A stark contrast to her mood at function with Elvis."

Celebrity Parade wrote, "Priscilla's been putting the pieces of her life back together, and handsome model Mike Edwards is giving her the support and love she needs."

We both got a kick out of reading the articles, but when I reminded her of how paranoid she'd been, she stuck to her guns, telling me that in the future she'd appreciate it if I'd check with her before talking to reporters about us. She wanted to be the one in control of her publicity. It was a game she knew well, and, besides, there was no denying the fact that she'd been taught by a master.

"No one could play the press better than Elvis," she said. "He used them to create a mystique. Never give them everything they ask for, he said. Always keep them hungry for more."

We decided to stop letting the paparazzi photograph us. Priscilla was concerned about getting overexposed in gossip magazines.

"From now on," she said, "we have to be much more selective."

When *People* magazine called, offering Priscilla the cover, we both readily agreed that this was one interview we should do. They promised Priscilla that there would be no questions about Elvis. They were interested in her new career and the new man in her life, me.

After one of our epic nights on the town, I woke up one morning feeling depressed and hung over and wishing I had more cocaine. But we'd gone through everything we had the night before. Priscilla lay sleeping beside me, and

I studied her reflection in the full-length mirror over the bed. Her complexion was pale and there were dark circles under her eyes. My face looked yellow and bloated, and I felt strange, deep pains in my abdomen. Why was I doing this to myself—and to her? I thought of the night we'd met and how radiant she'd looked. And even further back, to an earlier time when all I'd ever gotten high on was beer. Hangovers then were bad enough, but they were nothing compared to the mental anguish I felt after doing coke, the feeling of being eaten up inside. It was unbearable and I couldn't shake it off.

I took her in my arms and she murmured, "Are you okay?"

"Not really, baby. No more coke for me."

She hugged me and said, "I'm so glad. I couldn't tolerate what you're doing to yourself much longer."

"I want you to look good for that *People* cover next week."

"I want you to look good, too."

On the day of the *People* shoot, Priscilla, Lisa, and I started out early in the morning. The photographer wanted some shots around the swimming pool, and then we drove the Jeep to her manager's ranch, where the rest of the photos were to be taken, including some of us on horseback.

Lisa was more interested in the lollipop she was sucking on than posing for some photographer. She was wearing jeans that she'd outgrown. They'd been let down all the way but were still too short, because she was growing very fast.

At one point we were galloping along on our horses when Lisa began to have trouble with her mount. She broke into tears, crying, "Mommy! I can't hold him in!"

Priscilla was firm and wouldn't let her give up.

"You're a good rider, Lisa," she insisted. "Don't let the horse control you. You control *him*."

I didn't know why Priscilla was letting Lisa be in the photographs. She had been overly protective about Lisa's privacy, but, suddenly this was no longer so. When I saw the pictures later, they gave the impression of a loving family, and I realized that the new sense of security in Priscilla's life was making a big difference. Perhaps she was beginning to feel safe enough with us to leave some of her old habits behind, and hopefully, to her we were a family.

The Star got a hold of the photos from the *People* shoot and headlined "Priscilla Presley in Love: The King's Widow Finally Comes Out of Seclusion." They ran an intimate picture of Lisa, Priscilla, and me with the caption: "Lisa watches her mother and Edwards cavort in their private swimming pool."

On my birthday, Priscilla's surprise gift to me was a trip to the Monterey Peninsula for the Jazz Festival. She told me that her manager was in Monterey the same weekend and that he'd invited us to join him at Clint Eastwood's restaurant, the Hog's Breath Inn, on Saturday evening.

We arrived at the Hog's Breath late. Spotting her manager sitting at a table with a group that included Clint, we walked over to them. They smiled and shook hands, but no one offered to move over and make places for us at the table. We stood there awkwardly, wondering what the hell to do. Finally I took Priscilla by the arm and found another table nearby.

"That's your manager?" I said. "You've got to be kidding."

"Maybe it's our fault for being late."

At the Monterey Jazz Festival later that night, we were

all supposed to sit together, but again Priscilla and I were sloughed off to seats by ourselves.

Priscilla said, "This is why I never got into the business when I was with Elvis. He always told me the only place to be in the movie business is at the top."

"You're going to make it, baby, with me behind you all the way. I've made it to the top in modeling, and we'll make it together in show business. You'll see."

I took her back to our cottage that night, built a fire, and held her in my arms. We managed to salvage the weekend and had a great time the next day, renting a convertible and cruising the Seventeen-Mile Drive.

In the months to come, I realized I was the only one who could teach Priscilla what she needed to know to get her career off the ground. She looked to me for guidance on everything, and it made me feel good to be able to share my expertise with someone I loved. I taught her everything I'd learned in modeling about makeup and fashion, and she was especially interested in what I knew about European designers and their style. She had no distinctive look of her own and seemed to always need a man to give her one. With Elvis, she had mile-high black hair. While we were together, she lightened her hair, going from brown to a golden wheat color, giving her a much softer and more natural look.

I went through her closets and drawers, making her throw out more than half her wardrobe.

"First thing, get rid of all this polyester. Then throw all these old T-shirts out."

"But some of them aren't that old," she protested. "I like them."

"Get new ones! You've saved everything. I'll bet you even have clothes here from high school."

Her sheepish grin told me she had.

"Why do you save everything?"

"I guess because my father's that way. He never throws anything out, either."

I couldn't find a single designer outfit in her entire wardrobe, except for the few things she had designed herself that were left over from Bis and Beau, the Beverly Hills boutique she'd opened after leaving Elvis. She'd designed little lacy one-of-a-kind outfits for customers such as Barbra Streisand.

Priscilla was interested in my knowledge about fashion and even though I preferred my jeans, her enthusiasm sparked in me a renewed interest in clothes. I introduced her to Brandon Wolfe, a designer friend who'd run around with me and Ron Levin. He owned one of the first trendy boutiques on Melrose. It was called Savage Space, and it was way ahead of its time. Brandon said we dressed too conservatively. Priscilla loved his flair and immediately let him dress us in stunning outfits. Our favorite was his soft cotton white Willi Wear trousers, which he mixed with 1920s tuxedo jackets of thinnest white silk.

I'd been in front of the camera for many years and had helped many beginners become models, and it would be a piece of cake to get Priscilla started. When her longtime friend Tony Orlando invited her to appear on his TV special, Priscilla ran into some difficulties with her acting. They were in an ice-cream parlor and Priscilla was the soda jerk and Tony the customer. After the first take, she came over to me and said:

"I don't know what to do with my hands. I feel stiff and awkward, standing there."

"Make believe you're in the kitchen at home," I said.

I noticed a towel lying on the counter of the soda fountain.

"Take that towel," I said, careful not to let anyone see me directing her, "and use it as a prop."

"What do I do with it?"

"Wipe off the counter or pretend you're drying a glass."

When they started filming again, Priscilla took up the towel, and a whole new actress emerged, confident and poised. I'd always felt so secure with women that the chance of there ever being any kind of competition between us never occurred to me. I was the strong one, someone you could lean on. But as I watched Priscilla from the background, I felt a twinge of jealousy. I didn't like her being up there in front of the camera. I'd never before been involved with a woman who could upstage me. For the first time in my life I felt my masculinity threatened. I had deliberately taken a back seat to Priscilla and it made me feel angry at myself. She was forcing me to face the fact that maybe some things about my character were negative and holding me down. She had nothing but eagerness and positiveness about us, her family, career, and life in general. She was one hell of a woman. And I needed to make some changes in my attitude if I planned to fit into her world. There was still an area in me of distrust, of anger, of carrying a chip on my shoulder. I didn't like it and I wanted to get rid of it.

16

Nearing twelve, Lisa was beginning to blossom, and it was clear that she was going to be a beauty. She resembled Elvis to an extraordinary degree, and looked more like his twin than his daughter. She had the same hairline, eyebrows, and heavy lids. Her hair was light brown, like Elvis's before he dyed it black, and her eyes were pale blue. In the privacy of her room, she loved to listen to blaring rock 'n' roll. Dressed in black tights like her favorite singer at the time, Pat Benatar, she clutched a toy microphone as she sang along with the records and danced in front of the mirror. Occasionally Lisa played her dad's records, but when she did she always turned the volume down, as if keeping him to herself.

When I got home each evening, I often found her visiting in the servants quarters, watching the soaps with the live-in couple. She looked quite at home, curled up in their bed while the couple sat nearby on the sofa.

The live-in couple were very much a part of the family. Weekends they spent alone in their room, watching television and eating from the crates of fresh fruits and vegetables they kept stashed underneath their bed. Only in their mid-thirties, they rarely left the house except to take Lisa to school or to the doctor, run household errands, or drive to the country to restock our produce supplies.

They put up with me for about a year and then resigned, quietly explaining to Priscilla that there had been "too many changes" in the household and they no longer "fit in." Priscilla had been a vegetarian when she'd hired them, but I'd changed all that, convincing Priscilla that a little red meat was good for you. They didn't agree, and they disliked having to prepare meat dishes, which they'd had to do quite often since my arrival. They also objected to "too much socializing." Part of the problem was that Priscilla depended on the butler to be the man of the house, and when I moved in and took over I replaced him.

"It's great having someone who can fix things," Priscilla told me. "I love it that you're so handy. Where did you learn all that?"

"I learned it from running the motel in Florida."

"I know what you ran after at the motel," she said with a sly grin.

I was sad to see the couple go—I loved their cooking.

Lisa was distraught when she heard they were leaving. They'd virtually become her foster parents, and their down-home ways reminded her of the family she missed at Graceland. For a long time she was resentful, blaming me for their departure. Tears running down her cheeks, she said, "If you didn't drink so much around them, they'd still be here."

"Drinking a little wine didn't chase them away."

"That's what you think," she said, glaring at me like her dad.

Lisa loved the couple like family and didn't want any strangers taking their place.

"What am I supposed to do now?" she asked me. "Who have I got to talk to?"

She was just beginning to accept my moving in, and was upset over yet another change in the household. She continued to remind me that I was to blame for her losing the couple.

"I want to go back to Memphis," she said. "I don't like it here any more."

Graceland had been Elvis's sanctuary and he'd returned there regularly, just as Lisa wanted to do now. Elvis had kept his family together there throughout his life.

"Lisa, they wanted to leave anyway," Priscilla said

"No, they didn't."

"They preferred living in the country. It was a very hard decision for them to make, leaving you."

"They left because of Michael."

When Priscilla and I were alone one night, she said, "I'm very concerned about Lisa. She gets so attached to people, it's hard for her to let go. Since Elvis died, she really comes apart when she loses anyone."

It was a horrendous period for Lisa, who continued to grieve over her loss of the live-in couple. She was becoming more and more introverted. Priscilla and I were so wrapped up in each other and preoccupied with nightlife, being photographed, skiing, condo-buying in Colorado, charity events, boozing and having lost weekends together, that Lisa was constantly being left with her grandparents or with Priscilla's sister.

"Mommy," Lisa said, "can't you guys do something different than go out to dinner all the time?"

"What would you like to do, Lisa?"

"Go to Magic Mountain, or something fun."

"Let's have a barbecue at the beach," I suggested.

"That's still eating!"

"Oh, come on, Lisa," Priscilla coaxed. "It'll be fun. You can invite a friend."

We drove up the coast, the trunk loaded with food and sodas and beer, for a day of picnicking. Everything went fine for a while, until I started barbecuing and the wind came up, blowing sand all over the chicken. Priscilla, as usual, wasn't upset and tried keeping everyone's spirits up.

"Lisa," she said, "it's just a little sand. You can brush it off."

As we studied our charcoaled, sandy chicken breasts, trying to figure out how to eat them, the sky opened up and down came a rainstorm. We gathered everything up and ran for the car. I looked at Lisa and never before had I seen such a look of misery. I told her she was right: Magic Mountain would have been better.

She just said, "Huh, it's a little late."

In the car, Priscilla touched my arm and smiled at me. "I think you made a wonderful picnic, Michael. The potato salad was good." Priscilla looked back at Lisa and suddenly the two of them cracked up. They had something going between them that I never became a part of. They were so close. I envied it.

After a while, Lisa stopped coming out with us to restaurants. We fed her at home, and then dropped her at her grandparents' house. Priscilla didn't like leaving Lisa home alone, fearing kidnapping.

"Mommy, I'm big enough to take care of myself," she said. "You can leave me alone."

Priscilla finally consented to let Lisa stay in the house by herself. On evenings when we were going out, though, before we even got through the gate, Lisa would come running out, saying, "I think someone's in the house. I heard a noise."

I'd have to go back inside, check every room and closet, especially under the beds, before she was satisfied. When we'd come back, the whole house would be lit up like a Christmas tree. Lisa had turned on every light in the place. Lisa and Priscilla loved watching scary movies together, and Jason in *Friday the 13th* really had Lisa spooked.

Since Elvis's death, Vernon Presley, his dad, had been running the estate. As Vernon's health deteriorated, Priscilla was gradually taking charge. One evening down by the pool she told me, "There's no one else in the immediate family who can do it."

When she went to Graceland on business, I was left to look after Lisa. One night, while Priscilla was gone, we decided to take in a movie. It was a hectic evening on Hollywood Boulevard, full of traffic and tourists and Chicanos cruising in their low riders. Crossing the busy intersection near the theater, I took Lisa by the hand. When we reached the other side, I became aware that she hadn't let go of me. Who was this little person clinging to me, I wondered, causing me such mixed emotions? Before this, I'd always thought of Lisa as a second daughter, treating her like my own child. But now I was engulfed by a stronger emotion, and my heart leapt. After that night at the movies, Lisa and I grew closer. She started making up fond nicknames for me, calling me Merkly or sometimes Mickley.

Lisa attended a private school in Culver City, and since we hadn't yet replaced the servants, who normally drove her back and forth, Priscilla and I were alternating chauffeur duties. I loved seeing Lisa coming down the steps of the school to meet me, looking adorable in her school uniform—a short gray wool skirt, white blouse, and loafers with bobby socks—but she hated it, saying it looked ugly and felt scratchy.

Priscilla was sixteen when Elvis flew her to America from Germany, where her father was stationed in the air force. Later, when Elvis brought her to Memphis to live with him, he placed her in a Catholic school. She had to wear a uniform just like Lisa's. She didn't like it any better than Lisa, especially when Elvis teased her and continued to do so unmercifully. But it definitely turned him on, and the press came to refer to Priscilla as Elvis's "teen heartthrob" and "Live-in Lolita." Seeing Lisa mimicking grownup ways in her little-girl outfit, I could certainly understand Elvis's feelings.

Priscilla told me she was beginning to have second thoughts about a show business career, and wasn't sure she really wanted to have one. It wasn't coming fast enough, and she didn't like all the hassles involved in starting at the bottom. We both thought she'd be accorded special treatment as Elvis Presley's ex-wife, but she wasn't. The industry viewed her as just another ambitious actress. I tried everything to keep her from giving up. My own career was going full blast, and one day I told her about an orange juice commercial I'd just been cast in, where I was playing Rudolph Valentino. The director had me attend casting sessions while they chose a girl to play opposite me. He made the actresses do all kinds of seductive things in front of me, like belly dancing and sighing and swooning.

Relating this to Priscilla, I said, "You would have been

perfect for the job. You're sexier and better looking than any of those girls."

She visited the set and saw me working in my Valentino costume. On a break, we went back to my dressing room and I told her that we should really think about remaking one of Valentino's films. She and I would be perfect together. I took her over to the full-length mirror.

"Just look at that," I said. "Why do you think they cast me in this commercial?"

"You really do look like him," she said.

"Elvis played Valentino, didn't he?" I asked, lowering my head and peering at her from under my eyebrows.

"Yes, and he'd come home from the studio and keep his Valentino makeup and costume on all evening."

"How was the movie?"

"Another disappointment."

Since MGM hadn't let Elvis play his Valentino character dramatically on the screen, he portrayed Valentino for Priscilla at home, doing it the way he wanted to.

I can remember one morning when Priscilla had an appointment for a reading at Universal Studios. I drove her there, letting her off at Universal's infamous Black Tower, which strikes terror in the hearts of both actors and executives. A while later, she came out looking disappointed.

"How did it go?" I asked her.

"I did it, but my mind went blank. I got so nervous up there I froze in my chair."

"What did the casting director say?"

"He suggested that maybe I should study acting for a while. Then he asked questions about Elvis. I don't know why I bother."

"That's not true," I said. "Don't think that way. You have a lot of talent of your own."

I brought her with me while I was doing a TV shoot in Mexico City for a Mexican fashion designer. When we arrived on the location, I introduced her to my director, and later he asked me, "Is that the same Priscilla who was Elvis Presley's wife?"

When I told him yes, he said he'd like to use her in the commercial. That's what finally persuaded me that she'd been correct in thinking that Hollywood was only interested in her because of her connection with Elvis. I began to wonder if I too would soon be treated differently because of my relationship with Priscilla and the Presley name. I didn't tell Priscilla what he'd asked; instead, I told her he'd flipped over her blue eyes and wanted to use her in the commercial.

"I don't think I can," she said.

"It's not hard, and it would give us a chance to work together."

That argument helped, but she was still wavering.

"I wouldn't know what to do," she said.

"With me there, you won't have to worry about a thing."

Priscilla and I had a lot of fun shooting the commercial, and it was the first opportunity we had to work together. As a veteran model, I had years of experience in helping newcomers relax. Our first setup was in an outdoor café. Following the storyboard, I sipped my champagne, noticed Priscilla sitting at a nearby table, and gave her the once-over as a possible love interest. She had to respond to my come-on with a smile that said yes.

Priscilla was very stiff, trying to act elegant. To loosen her up, just before the camera started rolling I started bouncing around like a gorilla, making noises and scratching under my arm. It worked. Her laughter made her relax and look her beautiful, natural self. In the next setup, I was in a different suit. We were in a jewelry store and I was buying her a silver necklace. Again she stiffened. This time, I took her in my arms in front of the entire crew and whispered in her ear, "Don't think of anything but you and me. Just pretend this is real. In a way, it really is." The shoot went off without a hitch.

Afterward, Priscilla seemed to have new respect for me professionally as she became aware that being a successful model entailed something more than just being photogenic. There was also a craft to it, the ability to know your best angle, what works between you and the camera. You had to have the capacity to project energy, life, and sexuality. It was a matter of mood, spirit, attitude, and soul. It could be learned; I used it, I could teach it, and Priscilla knew it.

Before dinner that night, she presented me with a Barry Kieselstein-Cord snakeskin belt with an elegant sterling silver buckle the size of a child's fist. I could see her giving something like this to Elvis for one of his Vegas costumes. I knew she'd loved shopping for him, searching out one-of-a-kind accessories in boutiques around New York and L.A., but it was too dressy for me. Levi's and a T-shirt were more my style. Despite brief periods of fun with Brandon Wolfe's trendy clothes, I really disliked dressing up, since I had to do it all the time as a fashion model. But Priscilla was always after me to wear nice clothes. I loved her so I put on the belt, but it felt like an anchor.

Everybody on the shoot commented on it and wanted to know where I'd bought it. In anger I was tempted to tell them that it was one of Elvis's and that I'd had to promise Priscilla to dye my hair black before she gave it to me. I suddenly realized that since being with Priscilla, I'd started to change my attitude. I didn't mind that too much, knowing I had some rough edges. But when someone attempted to make me over completely, it did bother me. A feeling of claustrophobia swept over me, just like the time in the principal's office when he threatened me with the scissors. I got loaded at dinner, and that night I made love to Priscilla for hours, trying to drive every memory of Elvis out of her for good. "I'm me, and that's good enough, and no one is ever going to make me be somebody else"—that's what I was trying to show her. I wanted to make love to her as no one ever had before, fulfilling her so completely that she'd awaken the next morning a different woman, someone who wouldn't even be able to think of wanting to change me. Suddenly, Elvis and I were in conflict.

17

The day we returned from the Mexico shoot it was windy, but warm and sunny. It had just rained the day before. Priscilla had a meeting right away with her manager, and when she came home that afternoon, she was upset. She told me he was pushing her as a replacement on "Charlie's Angels," but she still wasn't confident enough to take on a starring role and she didn't think it was smart to begin her career with a show noted for its cheesecake appeal. Since that wasn't the direction she wanted to go in, she declined the "Charlie's Angels" chance, and we decided it was time for her to change managers. We selected a new one, who was a Scientologist.

He turned out to be aggressive and hard-nosed. I felt he was trying to take over her life, but his virtue was that he was tenacious and utterly relentless in his determination to make her a star. He and I locked horns immediately, both vying for Priscilla's time and attention. I saw him as a threat—he wanted to be involved in every area of Priscilla's life. At the same time, I respected his ability and his drive, and I knew that he would succeed in guiding Priscilla to stardom.

Scientology had first come into Priscilla's life during a lunch with John Travolta. John had raved about how Scientology had changed his life, helping him clean up his act and bolster his career. Wanting the same benefits, Priscilla had become a Scientologist, and she liked it so much she got Lisa involved also. Then, when Priscilla and I met, she told me about Scientology and asked if I'd go with her to CC (the Scientology Celebrity Center in L.A.). It would help us communicate better, she said.

"No way," I told her, proclaiming that I'd sworn after the marines that I'd never let anyone else control my life. Eventually, however, I went with her to please her. I fully expected to find a bunch of phonies and to expose them to Priscilla as such.

Instead, Scientology turned out to be a reaffirmation of my own philosophy of life. I'd always believed that there's nothing you can't achieve; all you need is faith and you can reach your full potential for greatness. It seemed to bring me and Priscilla closer together at first. Yet I was now beginning to see more clearly certain issues in our relationship that I resented. One night I was a guest with Nina Blanchard on Merv Griffin's show. After a few questions about modeling, Merv said, "Are you going to pursue an acting career? You certainly could be a leading man."

I thanked him, we chatted pleasantly for a few minutes, and then Merv leaned toward me intently.

"We hear you have a special lady, Michael," he said, "the lovely Priscilla Presley."

"That's true," I said, concealing my annoyance. I wasn't on that show to talk about my romantic life, and I understood at that moment how Priscilla felt, constantly being reminded that she was who she was because of Elvis. They were doing the same thing to me, and I didn't like it.

"Are there wedding bells in your future?" Merv persisted, looking at me coyly.

I chuckled along with the audience as Merv waited for my answer. I didn't have one. As I sat there I had to restrain myself from jumping up and down on the couch and singing, "You Ain't Nothin' But a Hound Dog," giving them what they wanted. Finally Merv shrugged, changed the subject, and the show continued.

I wanted to be taken for what I was, and resentment over being thought of as "Mr. Presley," known only for my association with Priscilla, gnawed away at me.

I found myself shortly after this on a print location in southern Florida. This was my first trip away from Priscilla in a while, and she wouldn't be joining me. That was okay with me, because I needed a little time to think over my situation. Though I enjoyed my newfound celebrity, it was a constant struggle to hold onto to my own identity, which was beginning to slip away.

I'd always liked southern Florida. It was balmy there, and I enjoyed relaxing at the cabana bars on the beach, sipping frozen Dacquiris in the shade of the palm trees. Normally I would have rung Priscilla the minute I checked in, but now for some reason I didn't want to.

The first night, the whole crew went out to dinner. Right away I noticed the photographer's assistant, a very athletic, wholesome, cute little blonde with a pleasant smile. I'll call her Casey. Usually photographers' assistants are men, since there's a lot of heavy equipment that has to be carried. Casey was the first female I'd seen in this job.

She was shy, and I was attracted to her, but I ignored her all through dinner. I didn't want to risk being unfaithful to Priscilla. I was surprised when Casey came along with me and Tony, the other male model, for a drink when we finished eating. We went to the bar on the beach, and Tony started talking to the girl next to him. Soon they disappeared together, and I was left alone with Casey.

We took our drinks and walked out to the water, kicking off our shoes.

"I've seen stories about you and Priscilla Presley in magazines," she said. "It must be wonderful to have such an exciting life."

"What I like is being here with you," I said with a laugh.

She looked at me in disbelief and said, "You do? I didn't think you even noticed me at dinner."

We strolled on, and when we came to a pier on the beach, we stopped under it.

"Look at the moonbeams between the pilings," she said. "They're playing hide and seek with one another."

I lay my jacket on the ground for us to sit on. My arm went around her shoulder, and I liked how firm and muscular she felt.

"You've really got muscles," I said. "It's kind of strange, feeling muscles and then seeing your blond hair curling on your shoulders."

She got embarrassed and pulled away.

"Please don't get me wrong," I said. "I really like you."

"You didn't have to say that."

I pulled her to me, we kissed, and then I made love to her.

When I got back to my hotel room late that night, I immediately regretted what had happened. I thought of Priscilla back in Beverly Hills and felt awful. I had sworn this would never happen.

I had to call her at once and confess. "It didn't mean anything," I wanted to tell her. And: "I'm sorry. It was a big mistake. It will never happen again."

But the phone in my room was dead, and when I went to the lobby, it was locked. I found a pay phone down the street. It was just after midnight West Coast time, and Priscilla told me she was about to go to bed.

"Have you been drinking?" she asked.

"Just a little. Why?"

"Because you're calling so late. I thought you'd be in bed by now."

"Can't you at least ask me how the flight was before nagging at me?"

"Why are you upset?"

"I'm not. I'm just tired."

"Well, maybe we'd better talk tomorrow, Michael. Good night."

After that I stayed away from Casey, concentrating on my work.

The next night we went to dinner, but Casey had to process the film we'd shot and clean the cameras, so we didn't see each other that day and the next. The last day I had the afternoon off and went swimming. Coming out of the water, I saw Casey.

"You've been avoiding me," she said.

"I didn't know what to say to you. It was the first time I was unfaithful to Priscilla."

"I understand about those things. I have a boyfriend back in New York. But life goes on."

We walked over to one of the little beach bungalows and sat down. We were alone except for an old couple walking along the beach looking for shells. I swore I wouldn't do anything else with this girl. Then her hands were on me.

"Being uptight doesn't suit your personality," Casey said.

The next thing I knew I was lying on my back, and she was pulling off my bathing suit. I looked up at the blue sky and felt her warm lips on me. I justified what was going on, thinking, This is all just part of the shoot. It doesn't really mean anything. It never has.

Flying back to L.A. I decided not to tell Priscilla. She didn't need to know anyway, since it didn't mean anything to me. Besides, I was still upset about her letting her Scientology manager take over all the things I wanted to do.

I was surprised when she picked me up at the airport in a white stretch limo. In the back were two dozen roses and a bottle of iced Dom Perignon. That weekend we had some friends over for a barbecue around the pool. After a few drinks, I took her aside and admitted to my infidelity in Florida. I couldn't keep it from her, but I tried to make it sound like a harmless flirtation.

Priscilla seemed casual about it at first, and she went on with the party as if nothing had happened.

About an hour later, the phone rang. Priscilla answered it and shot me a strange look, saying only, "It's for you."

It was Casey. I'd given her my number and said, "If you ever come out to L.A. and need help finding a job, give me a call."

Casey said she missed me. Priscilla was still standing next to me, confronting me. I didn't know what to do or say. Catching on, Casey said, "You can't talk now, can you?"

She tried to give me her number but I said, "Not now," and hung up.

"Michael," Priscilla said. "I'd like to talk with you."

She walked into the garden room. I followed her, and the

smell of the gardenias now sickened me. She turned and said, calmly, "That was her, wasn't it?"

I felt as if I were about to be fired. "Yes," I said.

"How dare you give her this number?"

"It's my phone number, too. What was I supposed to do?"

"Don't you ever let her call here again!"

"I was just going to help her with a job."

"Did you hear what I said?"

Priscilla returned to the party, leaving me alone. I watched her join some guests outside and resume her gaiety at once. After a moment she looked back at me, and there was disappointment in her eyes.

She had once believed in me and trusted me, but I had betrayed her. I wanted her to yell at me, get angry, throw things, anything other than being disappointed in me. But each time I tried to force the issue, she refused to talk about it. There was no further discussion of the incident. Now we had something between us that was threatening our life together. In the past, when there were problems in a relationship, and I was away on location, I'd always wind up having an affair. Natural, easy sex had been so much a part of my life for so long and was so much a part of being on location that it was difficult for me to give it up. I'd never felt anything wrong before, but now it was different. I wanted to be faithful to Priscilla and not fall back into old habits. How would I handle it? Go along with Priscilla's silence and do things her way? Or force a confrontation on the issue by giving her an ultimatum. Talk or I'll walk.

18

Days passed and the silence continued. Finally I decided to do things Priscilla's way and try to regain her trust. Maybe if I treated her as I had Lisa, and gave her some space, she'd end up coming to me when she was ready. We were in our second year together, and I couldn't imagine life without her. It worked, and one Sunday over breakfast, we just looked at each other and smiled, then I took her into my arms. "Michael, I love you, you know I do," Priscilla whispered, as I picked her up and carried her into our bedroom.

Priscilla convinced me to do the Purification Rundown through Scientology, and we did it together. This was to cleanse ourselves of any residue of drugs, alcohol, radiation, and other impurities. After the "Purif," I had a renewed outlook on life, and I suggested to Priscilla the idea of our doing a film together. It took weeks to convince her, but finally she agreed, and we decided it would be about the fashion world, and I'd write the screenplay. I put my own career on hold, turning down modeling jobs and commercials, and began working on the script. I was burning to take Elvis's place and I hoped that a more lucrative profession than modeling would help me fulfill the role as head of the Presley household. I knew I'd always have modeling to fall back on.

Each day I set up my work station down by the pool, with my typewriter, suntan lotion and a jug of margaritas or a bottle of wine. I was content getting sloshed, basking in the sun, and playing Ernest Hemingway, and the months slipped by in pleasant idleness.

In mid-afternoon I'd knock off writing and, slightly loaded, hop in the jeep and race over to school and pick up Lisa. On the way back I'd enthusiastically share with her all the writing ideas I'd had that day. Naturally, I should have been doing this with Priscilla, but she was still trying to get her career going. Much of her time these days was taken up with negotiations for a contract with Wella. I was beginning to prefer talking with Lisa, anyway. Her problems were small compared with Priscilla's and were easily solved. Lisa was satisfied just giggling and playing with me in the swimming pool.

Lisa seldom, if ever, had school friends over and she clung tenaciously to the little girl who lived next door. Though Lisa was a real sweetheart, a naturally warm-natured girl, she tended to be domineering, and this finally alienated even that one friend.

I didn't have many friends myself these days. I felt awkward bringing them around Priscilla's house, because she seemed uncomfortable the few times I did.

"There are so many things of great value around," she said. "Be careful who you bring over."

I assumed she was referring to Elvis's possessions, which were still all over the place. Priscilla and I would argue over this situation and I couldn't believe how mad we would get. But I sympathized with her and understood her concern. I felt just as protective about Elvis's things as she did, and friends had to be pretty special for me to share any of that with them.

One rainy Sunday afternoon, I came into the bedroom and discovered her going through the contents of the steamer trunk she kept at the foot of our bed. I turned to leave her in privacy, but she told me to stay.

I saw a packet of old letters of hers, neatly tied with ribbon, and some writings of Elvis with words to her. His handwriting was a childlike scrawl, similar to the way mine had once been.

Digging deeper into the trunk, Priscilla pulled out a little spiral notebook, the kind used in grade school. Elvis had used it to make notes to himself—errands he wanted his entourage to perform, a note about an airline reservation, and plans for a racquetball court.

There was a pile of Elvis's publicity photos, showing him in all the different periods of his career. One of the photos showed Elvis loaded down with rings and necklaces and belts, and I asked Priscilla if they were real.

"Most of them," she answered.

"I would love to have seen them," I said.

She went into her dressing room and brought out a jewelry box. We sat down on the floor in the bedroom, near the trunk, and Priscilla spread a great array of jewels out before us. I picked up a solid gold chain necklace, and Priscilla told me that Elvis had had it made especially for himself. The pendant was an old U.S. gold coin set in black onyx and inlaid with diamonds. There were many rings, clustered with precious stones, and there were also expensive gold and platinum watches.

"I want to give your mother something," Priscilla said, selecting a ring. I was surprised, but then I remembered how very much she'd liked Mom when they'd met in Florida. I was looking at a thin, elegant, gold watch lying on the carpet and knew I could have it or any of Elvis's jewelry if I wanted, just by asking for it. But I wouldn't let myself get trapped like that.

She handed me the ring she'd picked out for my mother. It was gold, with pink coral roses.

"This is one Elvis bought me when we were in Hawaii," she said. "It's very special to me. I want your mother to have it."

The ring became a catalyst in our relationship. I realized she was forgiving me for my infidelity, and I took her tenderly in my arms, thanking her.

We began to slip more into the secluded life that she and Elvis had led. We too were sealed away behind a wrought-iron gate from certain aspects of the world. I became accustomed to this unnatural existence—it gave me the feeling of invincibility, exempt from the normal rules of society. Once I had a taste of Elvis's charmed life, I began to prefer it. Later, my mother received not only Elvis's ring from Priscilla, but a new Cadillac Seville—from me.

During this phase of our relationship, we were both consumed by style, and loved getting dressed up to the hilt and going out and showing ourselves off. Priscilla discarded her old look. Picking up tips from makeup artists she'd met on shoots with me, she learned to use makeup like a pro, and was now beginning to find her own visual identity.

Living behind the big black gate was causing me to change more than I realized. Where jeans and T-shirts had once sufficed, I was now letting Priscilla pick out Armani linen suits and silk Valentino shirts for me.

On one of her rare days free of meetings, we were down at the pool having a swim when she said, "I want us together always. I don't know how I ever got along without you. I love you—your eyes, your smile, your beautiful nose, your mouth."

We climbed out of the pool and stretched out side by side on the lounges.

"I love you, too," I replied.

"What is it you're not telling me, Michael? I see something in your eyes."

"I'm just concerned about writing this script. It's taking longer than I thought. I don't want to give it up, but I'm running out of my savings."

"Maybe you should put the script aside, Michael. Like you once told me, you can't start at the top. You have to be willing to pay your dues."

"That's not what I want to hear. I get that from everyone else. Negativity—'You can't do it.'"

She got up to leave.

"Don't walk off," I said. "I need to talk to you."

"I have problems, too," she said, sitting down again. "It's hasn't been easy for me. Nothing was handed to me, either. Do you think living with Elvis was easy? I'm trying to get out from under all that and at the same time, deal with us."

"I sometimes forget, Priscilla. I'm sorry. I know it's hard for you, too."

I took her into the garden room. There's something very stimulating about a fight. It's both painful and erotic, stirring your emotions like a blender. That afternoon, lying on a large sofa, Priscilla and I made love more passionately than I'd ever remembered before. I believe it was then that we conceived a child. After we discovered that Priscilla was pregnant, we began lying in bed awake at night, trying to decide what to do.

"Do you want to have a child?" We both asked that question countless times. And:

"Are we ready?"

"How will Lisa take it?"

"What about our careers?"

Deep inside, a voice was crying out, "You must have it. You had Caroline because you don't approve of abortion. It's against your morals." But since then, I'd become confused. Life was no longer as simple or as clear to me. My intuition was telling me I didn't want to spend the rest of my life in this situation, living in Priscilla's shadow, in her house, surrounded by her things, oppressed increasingly by the Presley name.

Priscilla finally came to me and said, "I don't know what to do."

Even though I was part of the process that had created the baby, and my paternal impulses were urging me to have it, I heard myself repeating the advice Mom had given me when Grace had become pregnant.

"You'll do what's right," I said to Priscilla.

We stood in total silence, avoiding each other's eyes.

Later in the week, Priscilla asked if I would pick her up at the medical center on Beverly Drive at four o'clock in the afternoon. I felt sick. I knew as the father it was my responsibility to stop the abortion. We were both healthy people, but I said nothing. It was a sad and hopeless moment. A child might have given us the stability we lacked. It might have taken our thoughts off each other and away from our own personal desires.

As planned, I met Priscilla at the medical center. Attendants brought her out of a side entrance in a wheelchair. She was wearing dark sunglasses, but nothing could hide the desolate look on her face. It told me everything. I felt hollow, and I regretted that I hadn't taken responsibility. As I wheeled her along to the car, tears filled my eyes. I put my hand on her shoulder, realizing that there was nothing now more painful that could happen to either of us. We had aborted what no doubt would have been a great kid.

I carefully helped Priscilla into the passenger seat of the Mercedes and then rolled the empty wheelchair back inside the building. We drove home weeping, our hearts frozen in despair.

We were depressed for months. We couldn't seem to get the enthusiasm together to do anything. A distance had opened between us like a chasm, and it kept widening.

19

I hadn't worked for months, and I was rapidly going broke, my savings dwindling because of our extravagances. To get over our grief, we treated ourselves to holiday week-ends, dinners every night in a different restaurant, rampant shopping excursions, and cases of rare wines. Eventually we began to enjoy life again and started our third year together. But I could no longer live above my means and I shelved the screenplay I'd been preparing as a vehicle for Priscilla and me and went back to modeling.

Nina Blanchard was pleased that I was so charged up about my career, and one day I took her to lunch at St. Germain restaurant on Melrose Avenue, one of her favorite places. It was good to be back with Nina and hear all the news of my friends and associates in the fashion world. I hadn't realized how completely I'd dropped out, or how isolated I'd become since living with Priscilla.

"You should think about going to New York for a while," she suggested over coffee.

"I don't think that would be a good idea."

"Sweetheart," she said, "if it's Priscilla you're worried about, she'll wait. New tear sheets are what you need."

Nina saw through me. She knew exactly what was going on, and she didn't like the changes she was beginning to see in me. She'd known me long enough to see that I was no longer the old me and I was letting the Presley name go to my head.

"Let me think about it," I said. "In the meantime, let me try working here."

The next day she rang and said, "I have a trip to Australia for *Vogue*. There's no money to speak of, but Claude is shooting it and wants you to do him a favor."

I loved working with this gifted French photographer. Claude always encouraged my creativity and never balked at my ideas when we were shooting, no matter how far out my behavior. We always ended up getting exceptional shots.

I invited Priscilla to come along to Australia, and she excitedly accepted. I forfeited whatever small fee they paid and asked for a plane ticket for Priscilla instead.

When we got to Sydney, we were upset to learn that the clothes to be photographed had not been completed by the designers, and the shooting was canceled. Priscilla and I found ourselves stuck in our hotel. *Vogue* told us to stand by while they decided what to do next and not to leave our room. Early the next morning, we got a call from the *Vogue* office. They were sending us all to nearby Samoa to shoot a bathing-suit layout.

We soon discovered that we loved Samoa, and spent the next week on this lush Polynesian isle enjoying its gentle breezes, waving palms, and warm tropical waters.

Our guide, Aiaitue (pronounced *eye-eye-two-e*), took us to a remote village, which was to be our location for the shoot.

The natives cooked over open fires and lived in thatched huts called *felas*, and they were governed by a single chief. Aiaitue told us we needed to ask the chief for permission before we could shoot there and led us to him.

After introductions, Claude and I sat down with the chief and the village elders on the beach. Aiaitue conferred briefly with them and then turned to us and said, "You must pay ten thousand dollars a day. Otherwise, you will not be allowed to shoot."

"Ten thousand dollars!" said Claude. "That's impossible! It wouldn't cost that much to rent the Statue of Liberty!"

Aiaitue talked with the elders, explaining that we did not have ten thousand dollars. They looked at us very seriously, and then talked among themselves.

"How much can you pay?" Aiaitue asked Claude.

Claude shrugged and said, "I don't know—we have about two hundred and fifty dollars in our budget."

Aiaitue relayed this information. I expected to hear war drums, but instead, without a change in expression, the chief elder nodded his head and said, "Good, good."

Aiaitue told us later that a Japanese film crew had been through earlier and paid them ten thousand dollars for a two-week shoot, so we figured that ten thousand were the only words they knew in our currency.

A few days later, when Aiaitue was talking with Priscilla on the beach during a break in our shooting, he suddenly realized who she was. Claude had asked her something about Elvis, and Aiaitue made the connection, getting very excited. He called Elvis "the man who made the best music" and made her promise that when she returned to California she'd send him a signed photograph. It annoyed me that even on this far-flung South Seas island, we couldn't escape from him.

My shooting partner was a blond Swedish model named Trish, and I loved her natural abandonment. As soon as we arrived in the village, she stripped off all her clothes and went dashing into the surf. I tried to convince Priscilla to do the same. She refused, saying, "I'm not like her."

"I'm not saying you are," I said. "I'm just trying to get you to relax, to be like the natives."

"Leave me alone," she said. "I'm happy the way I am."

"Well, at least take your top off. You'll make everyone else feel uncomfortable if you don't."

"Michael, leave me alone."

"Be that way then, but I'm not," I said, pulling off my clothes and running out to the water nude to join Trish. I could feel Priscilla's eyes on my back like daggers.

Every evening we'd all have dinner together at Aggie Grey's Hotel, and I couldn't help comparing Trish's untamed beauty to Priscilla's coiffed splendor. An air of natural sexuality exuded from Trish that was as delicious as the sweet coconut milk of Samoa.

After dinner we all retired to the bar for brandies, and Priscilla excused herself and went to the ladies' room. Trish turned to me, her eyes sparkling.

"Just be who you are," she said, "and let Priscilla be the way she is."

Trish finished her brandy, laughed, and added, "Of course, I wish she wasn't here."

The next day when Claude and I were shooting a single, I saw Priscilla and Trish out in the water, swimming together. Priscilla had taken off her bikini top. Later that afternoon, after my shot, I joined her in the water.

"I'm sorry I was so mean to you yesterday," I said. "I just wanted us to walk naked on the beach together."

"I want to please you, but I'm not comfortable about some things."

"I know. But you shouldn't feel that way about your body. You have a better figure than any model I've ever seen."

Getting my camera, we went to a secluded section of the beach, overgrown with rich green foliage. Priscilla agreed to let me photograph her topless, wearing only a sarong slung low around her hips. She posed for me for a whole role of film.

"You look like you belong here in the islands," I said, "with your hair so wild and your breasts glowing pink from the sun."

She smiled, lying back seductively on a moss-covered tree trunk. We were truly in paradise.

Prophetic? Elvis played a character named Mike Edwards in one of his movies.

With my daughter, Caroline, at the motel.

With my inspiration, Caroline, in Pensacola. Memories like this kept me going during the dark times. (*Jimmy Hayward*)

The ad that started it all. (*Richard Noble*)

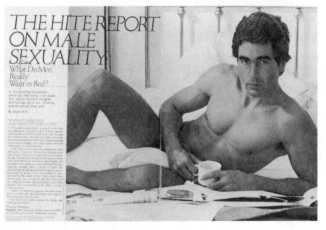

Cosmo. (Elyse Lewin)

With Erin Grey.
(*Claude Mougin*)

The woman I fell in
love with.

Fire Island Pines.

After clamming in the Pines.

A love as big as all
outdoors.

Lisa, Priscilla, and me.

Priscilla telling Lisa to control her horse. (*Frank Lieberman*)

Nick Rozsa

Caroline, Priscilla, and Lisa in Manzanilla, Mexico.

With Caroline, Daddy's big girl.

Priscilla, Lisa, and Miska.

Rehearsing with the cast of *Ballad of Lizard Gulch*. *(Barry King)*

In a Tokyo noodle joint.

The *Cosmo* layout. (*Elyse Lewin*)

Being intimate on the street in Beverly Hills. (*Ron Galella*)

In Brandon Wolfe outfits, with Brandon.

In New Orleans.

With Mom and Priscilla in Pensacola.

Priscilla played a major role in turning Graceland into a thriving business enterprise. (*Ron Galella*)

Caroline.

I loved to see Lisa smile.

Priscilla
posed for me
in Carmel.

Lisa, Caroline, me, Priscilla—Christmas dinner at Mom's.

A photo is worth
a thousand words—
we're together, yet
apart. One of our
last dates.
(*Ron Galella*)

Nick Rozsa

20

After Samoa's sparkling water, green mountains, and trade winds, L.A.'s concrete, smog, and traffic jams seemed like purgatory. We were relieved to get out of the city again when *Cosmopolitan* magazine booked us together for a layout on love and romance and took us up to Carmel-by-the-Sea on a shoot. We spent a week shooting in all the scenic spots along the Monterey Peninsula—Lover's Point in Pacific Grove, the Lone Pine on the Seventeen-Mile Drive, Nepenthe in Big Sur—and finished up the layout back in Beverly Hills at L'Hermitage hotel. *Cosmo* published our pictures in full color in two issues under the titles "Weekend Getaway" and "Love in the Afternoon."

Things were different in my career since my association with Priscilla. Clients and photographers now viewed me as a celebrity. The good part was that I could demand higher rates. The bad news was that many people felt I had changed and wasn't as uninhibited as I used to be, or as enthusiastic. The fact was, modeling no longer presented me with a challenge, and I disliked having to portray the unscathed, clean-shaven, all-American look most clients desired. I wanted to be doing something more meaningful. I was tired of having to look good all the time, fresh and smiling when I didn't feel like it. I wanted to be real and not worry about dark circles and puffiness under my eyes or bumps on my face. But since the bills kept coming, I kept accepting assignments. I was thankful to have Priscilla's constant reassurance that being a model was something to be proud of, and I didn't give it up.

Priscilla was in Memphis on business, and called me from Graceland late one night, after I'd gone to bed. She told me she wasn't able to sleep. The food at Graceland was so good she couldn't resist stuffing herself, and for dinner she'd had corn bread, hush puppies and fried chicken cooked the way only the cooks there knew how. After dinner she'd gone up to Elvis's bedroom. Since his death, it had been difficult for her to go in there.

"It was very strange," she said. "Nothing seemed changed. The bathroom, his towels, the bed—even the smell of his cologne. I felt as if he were still there. I couldn't look at anything without remembering. I had to leave—"

"Why did you go in there?"

"I wanted to get something."

"What did you take?"

"An ivory cane, a pair of his favorite blue pajamas, and some Polaroids and movies he'd taken of me."

"Was that the sexy stuff Elvis took of you and your girl-friend?"

"I wouldn't say it was sexy."

"Were you naked?"

"No. I had on panties and a bra."

"I don't believe you."

"Really. Elvis loved white cotton panties."

"Well, it was smart to get that back. You don't want to pop up in an X-rated movie some day. Can I see them?"

"Oh, I don't know, Michael. I'd be so embarrassed."

"It would be fun to watch them. Was Elvis in them, too?"

"He just enjoyed filming us."

"What did he have you doing?"

"We just kissed and hugged."

"I'd really love to see it."

"Maybe, if you promise not to get the wrong idea."

"I promise. Anyway, whatever you and Elvis did in your bedroom is your own business."

I always sleep in the nude, and I looked at myself in the mirror over the bed. I wished Priscilla and her girlfriend were with me now, in their white panties, rolling around on top of each other, their legs entangled and spread apart. It made me want to see Priscilla's teenage breasts, what only Elvis had seen in the privacy of his bedroom.

"Michael, are you there?" It was Priscilla, still on the phone.

"Yeah, baby," I said. "Hurry home. I miss you."

When she returned she showed me the cane, but wasn't ready to show me the film yet. The cane was black mahogany with a handle in the shape of an animal's head, carved from solid ivory, with gems for eyes. I enjoyed playing with it; it made me feel like a king.

Graceland was an increasingly important part of Priscilla's life. She didn't really want this involvement because she was trying to get away from the stigma of just being Elvis Presley's wife, but there was no one else to do it. She had to fly to Memphis for frequent meetings concerning Elvis's estate and, most recently, legal problems with Colonel Parker, Elvis's manager, and disagreements had arisen with RCA Records. She told me nobody knew what to do with the estate and there was talk of selling it because of expenses. Priscilla wanted to keep the house for Lisa, who, she said, would have been devastated to lose Graceland, the place of her earliest childhood memories, and her strongest link to her father.

Priscilla invited me to Graceland many times but I kept my distance, believing it was not right for me to get involved in that part of her world.

"I don't know what to do with this place," Priscilla said. "Tell me what I should do."

I wanted to help and give her suggestions but I wasn't a businessman and didn't want to jeopardize her position at Graceland. I knew she would trust my judgment and follow my advice, but I didn't want her risking anything because of me.

All the relatives in Memphis had seen my pictures in magazines and TV commercials, and when they phoned Lisa or Priscilla and I answered, they'd say, "We're looking forward to meeting you, Michael. When are you coming to Graceland?"

Morgan Maxfield, a close friend and longtime financial adviser, helped Priscilla with her investments, and she leaned on him for advice on all her money matters. Late one afternoon, a phone call came from Jack Soden, Morgan's associate. Priscilla and I were in the bedroom. She turned to me as she hung up, her face ashen.

"Michael," she said, "Morgan's plane went down."

We sat on the edge of the bed, and I tried to console her, but I was crying myself. Morgan was one of those rare, pure human beings who are always helping others. I liked and respected Morgan so much that I was never jealous of his past relationship with Priscilla.

"What am I going to do without him?" Priscilla asked.

Though I knew she was shocked by Morgan's death, I could see she was fearful of her own well-being, including her financial affairs.

Priscilla was a very smart woman. I'd hear her on the telephone with the executors, giving ideas and suggestions, but never once did I hear her being demanding or ordering anyone around for her own wishes. The other executors, including a judge, learned to respect Priscilla's input. It was her suggestion that the estate take on Jack Soden as an adviser. And did he ever advise! Consulting with Priscilla, he came up with an approach to run Graceland along the lines of the Getty Museum, the Hearst Castle at San Simeon, and Disneyland. Priscilla was torn about opening Graceland to the public, but I told her that Elvis would have been happy to share his home with those who loved him. Eventually she opened Graceland and soon it was out of the red and on its way to its present stature as one of the major and most efficiently run tourist attractions in the United States.

She came to me one day explaining that the executors and an attorney of the estate had arrived in town from Memphis. She'd invited them all out to dinner after their meetings that day.

"What restaurant should we take them to?" she asked me.

"How about the beach?" I suggested.

"I was thinking of something more like Chasen's."

"Priscilla, they live in Memphis and never get to see the beach."

"But they're always in suits."

"We'll pile into the Jeep, grab some beer, tell them to take their ties off, and go to that little restaurant on the sand in Santa Monica. They'll love it."

"Michael, these are distinguished businessmen."

"Trust me. Guys are guys, no matter what they do."

And, believe me, these men were no different. We not only had beer on the way to the beach, we had more to drink at the restaurant, and on the way back, driving through Westwood, they started flirting with some girls who pulled up beside us at a stoplight. They were joking and laughing as we sped off from the light.

21

My own antics were also getting out of hand these days, and a couple of nights later we went to a party at Sammy Davis Jr.'s house that wreaked havoc between Priscilla and me.

Sammy lived down the street, close enough for us to walk. Arriving at the party, we were curious to see the legendary guard who manned Sammy's front gate. Seeing the guard, we understood why. He was dressed in a black uniform with a low-slung pistol and highway-patrolman mirrored sunglasses, which he was wearing despite the fact that it was nighttime.

I took two glasses of wine from the bar, and we strolled outside to the pool area. Turning and looking back at the lively party inside, I saw a very large black man whose back was to us. He was dressed elegantly and was holding court to a group of guests who were listening to him intently.

"Besides Jacques Costeau," I said, "there's only one other person that I come close to idolizing, and it's Muhammad Ali, and I think that's him."

"I didn't know that," Priscilla said. "But you're right. That's him."

"I'll be right back," I said.

I'd already had quite a bit to drink that night, having finished a bottle of wine before we left the house. I wanted to shake Ali's hand, but I couldn't get through the group surrounding him, so I walked around and squeezed in behind a table and climbed up on a footstool. Holding onto a floor lamp, I leaned over the crowd, and suddenly I was eye-to-eye with Muhammad Ali. Someone accidentally—or probably on purpose—kicked the stool out from under me, and I fell to the floor at Ali's feet, causing a small commotion. Ali stepped back, looking down at me curiously.

Standing out in the garden where I'd left her, Priscilla heard the guests laughing and later told me, "I didn't have to guess twice. I knew it was you."

I brushed myself off and sat there on the floor for a minute, apologizing to the people standing around me. Priscilla had joined the group by then, and I smiled at her as I got up. She just shook her head as I led her to the bar.

"I think you've had enough to drink, Michael."

"I was just trying to shake hands with him."

"You made pretty much of a spectacle of yourself."

Somewhere in my mind I knew I was seriously out of control and should make amends to Priscilla and probably even to Sammy Davis, but I didn't. I was at war with myself, fighting to hold on to the old me. I was drinking to recover that lost person. I was also drinking because I didn't feel comfortable among all these show business moguls and movie stars and didn't feel like I was a part of them. I kept asking myself, Would I be here if it weren't for Priscilla?

After I downed a glass of wine at the bar, Priscilla told

me she was leaving; she wasn't going to stand around and watch me get drunker. She turned to go, and, though I wasn't really ready to stop drinking, I was unhappy at the party. I followed her out. Near the front door, I spotted Sammy talking with Liza Minnelli. Priscilla nodded politely and thanked Sammy for the party and exchanged greetings with Liza, introducing me to both of them. Then Priscilla walked away, but I remained behind, intrigued with Liza Minnelli. In all the pictures I'd seen of her she'd always had on mile-long eyelashes and excessive makeup. Tonight she was glowing, and I told her that I'd never seen a photograph of her that did her justice, that she was "much more gorgeous" in real life and that I would love to photograph her myself.

With those big eyes blinking and twinkling, she looked at me and said, "You're very kind. That would be very nice of you."

Squeezing her hand a little too long, I said, "I'll call you later and set it up."

I left, feeling very pleased with myself, and found Priscilla standing in the driveway. She was in a state of total outrage.

"I have never been so embarrassed and humiliated in my life," she said. She wouldn't talk to me on the way home.

"Priscilla, I can't be a phony like half those people in there," I said. "They can't be themselves. So what if I fell off a stool? Most of the guests would have loved to have been themselves like I was doing. You better learn to relax or you'll become like them."

"How are they, Michael?"

"They're—I don't know how they are, but I don't want to be like them."

"You went to the party, didn't you?"

"I made the party, Priscilla."

"No, you didn't. You disrupted it."

"They loved it."

"Did they?"

We walked along in silence the rest of the way home. At the gate Priscilla said, "I'm concerned about your coming to New York with me for the Wella convention."

"You're afraid I'll get drunk and embarrass you, aren't you?"

"It's my first press conference for Wella, and I'm very nervous about doing it. I appreciate the support you always give me, but nowadays I never know when you're going to drink too much."

"I've never screwed up any of my work. I give you my word, I won't screw up yours."

So I went with her for her first major shoot in New York. Wella put us up at the Regency Hotel on Park Avenue, which became Priscilla's favorite Manhattan hotel. Her press conference went well, and later we were interviewed and photographed together for the cover of *Interview*. *Interview's* publisher, Andy Warhol, personally conducted the interview during a lavish dinner at Quo Vadis restaurant. Later in the week, Andy continued the interview at Regine's nightclub.

"I've read about your dancing in the *Midnight Globe*," Andy said to me. "Are you and Priscilla going to dance tonight? I hope so. Gudonov is joining us later. He's the Russian ballet star defector. Maybe you could dance together."

Andy was curious about our sex life, and asked, "When did you have your first sex?"

Priscilla turned to me and said we'd better be careful.

"I don't like sex, myself," Andy said.

"I think sex is everything," Priscilla said. "I guess unless you're with the right people it can really be bad."

We wound up the interviews at a catered luncheon in the Factory boardroom a few days later, and Bob Colacello joined us.

"Do you find it hard to juggle simultaneous careers?" Bob asked.

"We have to work at it all the time," Priscilla said. "I'm usually the silent one in our relationship. Often Michael will tell me that I should talk more, get it out more. I really can't imagine myself being like that."

Andy Warhol said, "What's going to happen when Michael becomes a famous movie star?"

"Then I'll become more quiet," Priscilla said.

Andy had a photo shoot set up with Barry McKinley, a flamboyant Australian photographer renowned for shooting *GQ* and for being a real perfectionist. He'd been known to reduce male models to tears, but Barry and I had always worked together smoothly. He had a penthouse apartment down in Greenwich Village, and the natural light from his skylight and windows was ideal for photography. Barry positioned us by a window, where the reflection of the sun from the Hudson River was creating the most incredible golden light.

Barry examined Priscilla's face, inspecting it from every angle, and then shrieked in ecstasy.

"I would kill for those bones, darling," he told her. "Your features are so symmetrical. It's positively inhuman to be so flawless."

Then he turned to me and took my face in his hand.

"Absolutely heroic!" he exclaimed. "Such animal sensuality! So fierce and penetrating!"

He leaned in close to me, as if to kiss me, and then screamed and said, "Forgive me, Priscilla!"

Before pulling out his Nikon that day, he shot dozens of Polaroids, figuring out exactly how he wanted to photograph us. Sometimes, frustrated, he'd turn on his assistant and berate him. Then he'd turn back to us, purring flattery. Underneath all Barry's campiness was a true master. He created magic, painting with light and shadow, highlighting an eroticism in our faces that no one else had ever captured.

After the shoot, Priscilla returned to L.A. alone. I had to fly to Mexico for a catalog booking in Manzanillo. When we said good-bye at the airport, Priscilla thanked me for helping her through her first big fashion shoot.

"I'm glad you were there for me, Michael," she said. "I couldn't have done it without you—Wella, the Andy Warhol interview, our shooting. I'm so happy with us again, but why do I keep having this uneasy feeling that it's not going to last?"

"Don't worry about that, Priscilla. It's just the depression that always comes on after a shoot. When we're both back in L.A. next week, let's get into an acting class, like we talked about. I think we're both ready now for bigger and better things."

She put her arms around my neck and whispered, "I still worry about you when you go away from me."

"Why don't you join me in Manzanillo after the shoot? That way, you won't worry."

"Okay, but promise me you won't run off with a pretty senorita before I get there."

"I won't, I promise," I said, laughing. "I'll run off with all of them."

As my plane took off, I still had the warm, loving feeling we'd shared the past week. I didn't want anything to change us, but I too had an uneasiness, a little doubt somewhere in my thoughts, that neither Priscilla nor I was ready or strong enough to hold us together or to fight the pressures on us individually and together. Maybe our goals were too different. And perhaps we'd met at the wrong time.

22

This was the third trip I'd be doing with Gimbel's. They told my agent that I was being rebooked because not only did they like my all-American happy-father looks, but they'd always found me reliable and easy to get along with.

I arrived in Manzanillo for the week's shoot and checked into my hotel. Priscilla would join me in a few days, and I was looking forward to that. She'd told me she loved the frequent traveling we'd been doing since we'd met and was always eager to pack a bag.

I felt revitalized, having modeling jobs back-to-back again. And for once, I could relax—my shooting partner was a man, and I wouldn't have the temptation of a lot of beautiful females to deal with.

On the night before the final day of shooting, I decided to go with the guy I was working with to the disco in the hotel for one quick drink. I was determined to have an early night so I'd be refreshed for the sunrise cover shot the next day. But I let my buddy convince me to have one more drink.

"It's your last night before Priscilla comes," he said. "You'd might as well have some fun while you can."

Staying at the bar turned out to be a big mistake. After another shot of tequila, three cute Mexican girls sitting at a table near the dance floor caught my eye. I started dancing with the most flirtatious of the three, and she told me they were university students from Guadalajara. They were glad to have a break from their studies, and this was the first night of their vacation.

Back at the table, I started calling them the Three Senoritas. After more tequila we danced together, two of us, then three of us, then all of us. When we yelled at my buddy, urging him to join us, he said he didn't like dancing.

The girls loved me spinning them around to the strains of "La Paloma Blanca" and singing at the top of my voice. Finally, a slow song came on, and we returned to our table. I told my buddy I was ready to go. The senoritas looked disappointed, and the flirty one put her hand on my arm.

"We saw you in *Cosmopolitan*," she said. "When you first walked in, we recognized you, and I told my girlfriends, 'That's Priscilla Presley's new boy-friend.' "

Obviously she'd meant it as a compliment, but it irked me. Even these young women were seeing me only as Priscilla's boyfriend.

My buddy leaned in close. "I'm heading back," he said, "but if I was you, I'd stay. Looks like you can take your pick. Priscilla will never know."

I winked at him and ordered a bottle of champagne.

Leaving us, he said, "Don't forget your wake-up call. They want to do that sunrise shot."

After he left I continued partying with the three senoritas until closing time. Then I escorted them back to their bungalow. We were drunk, and they invited me in to get even drunker. After a while, two of the girls went to their room, and the flirty one and I went to her room and made love.

Afterward, she fell asleep, and I crept out of her bed. As I was leaving the bungalow, I glanced into the room where the other girls were sleeping. They were lying in twin beds, separated by a partition. I crawled into bed with the girl nearest the door, thrilled at the chance of making love to two different girls on the same night. At first the girl was reluctant, but after one kiss she changed her mind.

We made love, and then she disappeared into the bathroom. Waiting for her to return, I heard the third senorita stirring on the other side of the partition. I thought, Why not? Three is my lucky number anyway. I got out of bed and walked over to the last senorita. I looked down at her, lying there peacefully, gazing back up at me. I started to slip between the sheets with her but suddenly asked myself, What am I doing? I kissed her on the cheek and said good-night, heading for the bathroom. Reaching for the faucet, I tripped over the other girl. She'd passed out on the floor. I carried her back to her bed and tucked her in.

I felt desolate as I stood there in the soft light of dawn, looking down at the two sleeping girls. I remembered another lonely dawn—the time I'd been on a shoot in São Paulo, roaming the streets after a night of partying. I'd been out dancing, and my date had left me for a Brazilian. At daybreak I found myself in the middle of the open-air marketplace, which was just beginning to come to life. Passing a café, I saw my date and the Brazilian having some espresso. For a moment I spied on them. Evidently she was happy with him.

I turned and walked away, and a few moments later, a rotten odor almost knocked me over. Looking around, I saw hunks of meat, carcasses swinging from hooks with flies crawling all over them. It suddenly came to me I was wasting my life. I had somehow missed the whole point, and the real me was buried away somewhere, going to waste and rotting, just like that meat up there.

Leaving the three senoritas, I started walking back to my own bungalow. Suddenly I remembered that we were supposed to do a sunrise shot this morning, and I ran back the rest of the way, arriving breathless. My buddy was already up and dressed.

"You must have had a big night," he said. "You look like hell."

I splashed cold water on my face, and we rushed to work. When we arrived at the location on the beach, the client, photographer, art director, and assistants were fuming. The sun was already up, and it was now too bright for us to shoot. For the first time in my career, I'd caused the cancellation of a shooting.

I had always taken pride in my reputation as a professional, which I'd just trashed. I cringed as I heard the photographer say, "It's a wrap," and order his assistant to pack up the equipment.

I didn't have to ask—everyone's look of disappointment and anger told me I'd never work with them again.

Now I faced another dilemma. Priscilla was arriving on the afternoon flight. I wanted to get out of there, away from the senoritas, the Mexican sun, and the wreckage I'd caused. Another thought occurred to me: What would I say to the three senoritas if they saw me with Priscilla?

I felt like an asshole, and I was. What had made me get drunk, spend the night with those girls, and cause the cancellation of the shoot? Something in me was becoming unmanageable, and in my heart I knew these actions were trying to tell me something.

23

I greeted Priscilla at the airport clutching two margaritas that I'd bought at the bar, and I kept the booze flowing throughout the weekend. I managed to dodge the three senoritas, and we had a great time waterskiing, eating grilled lobsters, and renting a Jeep and driving around, exploring every nook and cranny of the town. After a few days Priscilla got a call from her manager urging her to come back. He had a lot of prospects lined up for her.

On our last night in Manzanillo, we hit every cantina in town. The next day, when we woke in the middle of the afternoon with pounding headaches, we decided it was time to go home and seriously dedicate ourselves to acting careers.

Returning to Los Angeles, we enrolled in Milton Katselas's acting class, which Priscilla had heard of through Scientology. I'd heard about Milton when I'd first moved to New York years earlier. I was fresh out of Pensacola and very naive. I'd been working out at the YMCA one evening when a guy approached me in the shower, identifying himself as a producer. Later, getting dressed, he eyed me as I dried off. "I'm making a movie and I'm about to cast the lead," he said. "You have just the body I've been searching for." I was elated. I knew I was going to hit it big and take New York by storm, but I didn't think it was going to happen this fast or in this fashion. I felt like a hustler, standing there naked and being appraised by another man. When he asked where I got my build from, I told him the marine corps. His eyes lit up at the mention of the word *marine*. He handed me his card, making me promise I would call him. "This isn't a joke or a game," he said. He wouldn't leave until he got my word that I'd call. A few days later, in his elegant East Side apartment, he auditioned me for the lead in his forthcoming movie based on a Tennessee Williams short story, "One Arm." His assistant told me the starring role was an ex-sailor who had lost his arm in an automobile accident shortly after discharge from the service. He'd then drifted into hustling and ended up in jail, where a priest befriended him and fell in love with him. The assistant then asked me to get completely undressed, since the scene I'd be doing was "the nude scene in jail." Once I was nude, he pulled out a role of adhesive tape and told me, "I have to tape your arm behind you, completely out of sight." After I read the scene, countless times, and in many positions, they told me I was great and they wanted me for the role and that the director of the film was going to be Milton Katselas. "As soon as Milton gets back in town," they promised, "we'll have you meet him." I got a few phone calls from them after that, telling me not to be impatient, that Milton was tied up, but the project was still on. Then one day came the message that the movie was "on hold." I never heard from them again.

Now, years later, when Priscilla and I started attending Milton's class, I asked him, "Did you ever have anything to do with Tennessee Williams's 'One Arm'?"

"Yes," he replied. "I vaguely remember something about that project. Tennessee is a friend of mine. Why do you ask?"

After I explained, he laughed and said, "I remember those two guys. They were real characters." Milton studied me for a minute and said, "You might want to do something from Williams's *Glass Menagerie* for the class."

When it came my time to perform a scene in class, I followed Milton's suggestion and did the opening and closing monologues from *Menagerie*. These are spoken by the character Tom, who also narrates the play. I related to Tom, because we'd both been deserted by our fathers, who'd left us with nothing but photographs and haunting memories.

Priscilla told me she wanted to observe the class for a while before she did her scene.

Meanwhile she landed her first TV series, "Those Amazing Animals." She and costars Burgess Meredith and Jim Stafford talked about the animal kingdom, bringing on creatures from every corner of the world—from anteaters and rattlesnakes to tarantulas and elephants.

One night, when the "guest star" was a tarantula, the trainer asked Priscilla if she wanted to hold it. She grimaced, but gamely stuck her hand out. The big furry spider cautiously crawled into her palm, sat there for a moment, and then continued up her arm, disappearing inside her blouse. The camera was running, and Priscilla, a real trooper, didn't flinch. It was a live show in front of an audience, and all the women gasped and held their breath.

"Don't worry," the trainer told her. "He likes the warmth of your body."

I was impressed because at home she and Lisa often came running to me to rescue them from some harmless, tiny spider in the bathtub or sink.

"Don't kill it," Priscilla would say. "Take it outside."

I'd have to pick it up with tissue or toilet paper, careful not to hurt it. Once I had it in the tissue, I'd chase after Priscilla and Lisa, who'd scream and run away.

Standing backstage that night at "Those Amazing Animals," I couldn't believe this was the same woman. Her determination and ambition were so great that she'd overcome her squeamishness. The girl who'd been in Elvis's shadow for so many years was beginning to shine on her own.

In the coming months, hosting this full-time TV show began to take up most of her time. In addition her manager was diligently trying to land a dramatic role for her, and kept her busy meeting producers. Now that she was constantly preoccupied with the show and her manager, she had very little time for acting class. Often I went to class alone, but Priscilla assured me she was still interested in further dramatic training and would attend when she had the time.

Where Priscilla and I had once been inseparable, it was now Lisa and I who were together almost every day. Since I was the closest thing Lisa had to a father at this troubling adolescent time of her life, she turned to me for love and support, and for simple things—trips to the drugstore, money, or to put a movie on the video for her. She demonstrated her appreciation by making ready-to-bake cookies and leaving them on the kitchen table. Soon I found I was looking at my watch, waiting for Lisa's school to let out, just as Elvis had once eagerly awaited Priscilla's return to Graceland from school each day.

Like her dad, Lisa was an avid acquirer of things. Elvis had scrupulously kept a cigar box full of various items— wood-tipped cigars, Tareyton cigarettes, a bottle of Dristan, Contac, Sucrets, emery boards, gum, gloves and sunglasses—and he wouldn't go anywhere without his box. She got attached to things in the same way, collecting everything from pills to rubber erasers, pencils, every color of pen and marker for sale, and Hello Kitty accessories.

I began feeling guilty about not spending more time with my own daughter, Caroline, who lived with her mother in Florida. I wanted her to come and live with us, and Priscilla and I discussed it. It was a difficult decision to make, and we finally reasoned that it would be unfair to Grace, my ex-wife.

"I wouldn't let Lisa live away from me," Priscilla said, "and I understand your feelings for Grace and her relationship with Caroline."

I was torn between my love for Priscilla and Lisa on the one hand and my obligations to my own daughter on the other. I started calling Caroline more frequently and tried to arrange my working trips so that I could stop off in Florida and visit her. Caroline was thrilled to have more of my attention, and I was happy that we were growing closer as she entered her teenage years.

Lisa was almost thirteen, and both of us were taking second place to Priscilla's career. Priscilla tried to be an attentive mother but there just wasn't enough time. She was beginning to like being in the spotlight and all her energies were focused on herself and her career. Like a flying wedge, she and her manager were going all out in their drive to make her a star. The two of them were so dedicated in their quest that I stood back and let them have at it.

By the end of the summer, Lisa's embraces seemed longer and closer every time we played together. I would ask myself, am I beginning to hug her too close? I enjoyed her affections, but, like every father who has ever seen a beautiful daughter through puberty, I found it difficult to keep a grip on my emotions. The fact that Lisa was not my blood kin didn't make it any easier.

Lisa was interested in my photographing her. I'd taken numerous pictures of her mother, and Lisa had often hinted that she'd like some of herself. As a model, I was well aware of the rapport that can develop between photographer and subject and was reluctant to photograph Lisa. We were close enough. But late one afternoon when I'd brought her home after school, I was in a mood for shooting some photos, and the light in the garden was soft and perfect for head shots. I dressed her up in one of her mother's vintage satin gowns, leaving the neck unbuttoned and letting the dress fall loosely about her shoulders. Pushing back her hair, I placed a big-brimmed 1920s hat on her head, with a floppy flower on top. She looked adorable.

She acted bashful and self-conscious, telling me she didn't want the servants to see us, so we went down to the far end of the pool, away from the house. I had her sit cross-legged beside the fountain.

"I don't know what to do, Mickley," she said.

I snapped off a rose and handed it to her.

"You don't have to do anything," I told her. "Just play with the flower."

Sitting down opposite Lisa, I looked at her through the camera, and as I began shooting I studied her features carefully. Her blue eyes were replicas of Elvis's and there was that touch of flatness about her nose, but it was her lips that enchanted me—small and full and petulant, like her dad's. I arranged her hair so that a few golden strands fell down, glowing in the sun. When I looked back at her again through the camera and continued shooting, she put the flower between her teeth and grinned at me. I had captured her.

"You're so pretty, Lisa," I said, my heart melting.

"Shut up, Merky. Don't be silly. I'm not pretty."

"You are, too, Lisa."

"No, I'm not. I'm funny-looking."

I heard the electrical click of the big iron gate as it opened in front. Willy and Ninja, our Dobermans, had been lying next to us, warming themselves in the late afternoon sun, and now they jumped up and ran to greet Priscilla. Through the shrubbery, I saw her white Mercedes pulling into the drive.

"We'd better stop now," I told Lisa. "Let's go meet your mother."

Priscilla met us as we came back into the house.

"What's going on?" she asked.

"I was taking some pictures of Lisa," I explained.

"Did you put that makeup on her?"

"Just a little bit—to blend her complexion."

"I see. Lisa, you'd better go to your room and do your homework."

As soon as Lisa left us, Priscilla's jaw tightened and her eyes turned that ice-blue color that told me she was livid.

"Did you have fun with my daughter, Michael?"

"She's lonesome, Priscilla. She doesn't have any friends to play with besides me. She's thirteen years old and she should be over at girlfriends' houses after school, not hanging around here by herself in this big, empty house."

"Aren't you a little old for her?"

Up until that moment, I'd accepted my feelings for Lisa as perhaps slightly more than normal affection. But the scene Priscilla had just created now made me feel as if I'd been caught red-handed. I was trying to be Lisa's father, brother, and friend, while fighting my attraction to her. I felt Priscilla was feeling threatened by her own daughter.

The next day Lisa asked me, "When can I see my pictures?"

The photos turned out beautifully. Lisa looked touching, her eyes warm, and she had an impish grin. When I asked Lisa what she thought of them, she obviously wasn't impressed.

"They're okay," she said, shrugging her shoulders.

She didn't ask me for any. I figured she wanted to look glamorous and grown-up, like the photos I'd taken of her mother. I wanted to take more pictures of Lisa, dress her up and make her look like she wanted to. But then, who knows what a teenager wants. I pushed that thought aside and put my camera away.

24

Priscilla finally decided to take acting lessons seriously.
She moved easily in any crowd. Like Elvis, she'd learned
to draw attention to herself in subtle ways, with a seem-
ingly natural, unaffected grace. She was becoming a full-
fledged glamour girl. Her hair, makeup, and clothes were
always perfection. But in acting class, it was a different
story. You had to leave your facades, images, and attitudes
outside. None of that mattered. Mercedes, diamonds,
beauty, prestige, even money won't get you anywhere in
the theater. Once onstage, what matters is your ability to
reveal yourself and let the audience see who you really are.
In other words, you have to be willing to make an ass of
yourself.

In a key exercise called Song and Dance, the student has
to stand in front of the class, perfectly still, and perform a
song a capella. While singing, the student also must carry
out various instructions from the teacher, such as skipping
around the stage, marching, disco dancing, crying, laughing, and bumping and grinding while acting sexy. The

objective is to break through your deepest inhibitions and fear of humiliation. As excruciating as it was to do, it was even more painful to watch the other students struggling through it, all of us making fools of ourselves. At times you wanted to cry for them, and at other times you couldn't stop crying for laughing so hard. But the transformations brought about by this exercise were phenomenal. All of a sudden the act that you'd used all your life to get by on wasn't needed any more. You'd tapped into that special quality that made you unique.

Song and Dance went completely against Priscilla's principles. I remember the first time I saw Milton Katselas put her through the exercise. That evening, preparing for class, she couldn't eat a bite, telling me she was so nauseous she was afraid she was going to throw up at any moment. She kept looking for excuses to cut class, but I was adamant, telling her, "I'll be there with you. Just glance down at me. You can do it."

I'd done the exercise myself and knew the terror she was feeling. But I also knew it would be good for her, and I couldn't wait to see her up there on the stage, especially when she had to start bumping and grinding. She'd told me she wouldn't do that, no matter what. I knew that she was reluctant to even wrinkle her forehead, much less bump and grind. She told me that Elvis had thumped her brow so hard every time she wrinkled it that she'd stopped because it hurt so much. Of all the things she told me about Elvis, this was the only one that made me want to kick his ass. He'd really thumped her hard, as if he was checking a melon for ripeness.

That night on the stage, Priscilla was in full command of her voice as she skipped and marched and sang. Then it happened.

"Disco!" Milton commanded. "Shake yourself around!"

Priscilla started dancing but couldn't lose control.

"Let yourself go! Sing louder!"

I could see she was fighting back tears. I felt for her. She was so elegant it went against nature to see her doing this. It was as if the Mona Lisa was suddenly asked to scream. Milton, however, did not let up on her. He knew the problems actors faced when they had to express certain feelings and gently coaxed her to continue. Trusting Milton's guidance, she slowly began to move her hips, determined to break through all her barriers. After a few minutes Milton let her stop. Applause broke out in the class, and I saw the biggest grin on Priscilla's face I'd ever seen, partly from satisfaction but mainly from relief that the ordeal was at last over. She walked off the stage, fast, and came over and sat down next to me.

"You were incredible," I said, "especially at the end when you smiled. You have such appeal. Everyone else could see it, too."

She squeezed my hand. "I've never felt my heart beating so hard in my life."

She told me later she so desperately wanted to be a good actress. I immediately started looking for a scene for us to do together in class. After a few more months of watching me do scenes, she agreed to do *Rain* with me.

Priscilla played the prostitute Sadie Thompson and I enacted the Reverend Davidson, who tries to save Sadie's soul but ends up falling victim to his own lust. I thought playing a South Seas hooker would help Priscilla continue to break through her shyness and reserved behavior.

Priscilla did very well in "Rain," and, in all honesty, she stole the scene completely away from me. I was happy she did. The class loved us, and our fellow students couldn't believe it was Priscilla they were seeing. Milton said it was a big step for her. He then told me, "I don't want you two working together for a while. Michael, you're spending half your time watching out for Priscilla instead of concentrating on your own work. But I commend you both for a good piece of work."

As the months went by and her scene work improved, I suggested we do another scene together. But this time, I told her, why not take a big risk? I'd just read a new play, and it hadn't been done in the class before. She asked me what it was called, and I told her *Porno Stars at Home.* I wanted us to do the first scene, which opened with a monologue spoken by the lead, Sarah Bernhardt, a porno queen. Sarah was giving herself a birthday party to announce her retirement from the porno world because she was pregnant. My character, also a porno star, had got her pregnant during their last picture together.

Priscilla's monologue started out with Sarah Bernhardt announcing that she didn't want to hear any foul language at her birthday party, specifically the words *cock, cunt, dick-licker, cuntlapper, dork, dang, snatch, balls, fuck,* or *asshole.* Priscilla's first reaction was, "You've got to be kidding."

"Just give it a try," I said.

She did, and as I worked on the monologue with her, I noticed an interesting phenomenon. Not only did she seem right at home in this part, easily handling the dirty dialogue, she made witty remarks to me about the characters having to do all that "licking and lapping and dorking and danging."

Priscilla had two personalities, and when she allowed herself to divorce one from the other, she could play a perfect prostitute. When I complimented her on how quickly she was progressing, saying how impressed I was with the character she was creating, and that she was very believable, she told me, "I'm a Gemini. There are two of me."

Trouble started the minute Priscilla and I began doing scenes with actors of the opposite sex. Everything had gone along fine until then. The class had brought us closer, giving us a common pursuit. Now it drove a wedge between us.

I'd been in and around show business long enough to know that you shouldn't mix business with pleasure. Anytime I broke this rule, which was quite often, I usually found myself in hot water.

Priscilla, however, was a newcomer and couldn't know this. When a smooth operator who was clearly after her body told her that most everybody in the class was having affairs with each other and that the girl I was working with was notorious for sleeping around, she seemed to believe him. She knew from rehearsing with me that I didn't fake anything in my acting, including love scenes.

"If you're going to kiss, then kiss. Make it real," I told her.

"You mean all the way?" she asked.

"No, not all the way. There's a fine line. You don't have to actually sleep with someone to make it look like you're sleeping with them onstage. Believe it yourself, and the audience will, too."

The seed had been planted though, and I don't think Priscilla thought I was telling the truth.

One night in class, when she and her acting partner were doing a love scene, they went into a long kiss. Many of the students turned to me to check out my reaction. I maintained a deadpan expression but I was hurting inside. This was the first time I'd witnessed Priscilla in the arms of another man. To make matters worse, she was allowing him to French kiss her. I was surprised since she'd complained to me that his breath always smelled like an ashtray. I'd told her to be real, and by God, she was. I had to keep reminding myself that this was an acting class; that kind of stuff didn't matter. So I dropped it.

But in the coming weeks, I couldn't ignore persistent signs that something had come between us. Priscilla was distant and cool with me. When I became ardent and insistent, she offered excuses. This had never happened before, and it was a clear sign to me.

Priscilla was scheduled to go to Japan to participate as a judge in the Tenth Annual Tokyo Music Festival, and she was to be accompanied by her manager. I wanted to go, too, and told her how much I loved Tokyo.

"I don't think that would be a good idea," she replied. "What I really think we need is a little time apart."

"We don't need time apart," I said. "We need time together."

"I just want to be on my own for a while."

"Your damn manager's going with you. That's not being on your own."

"You're making me nervous."

I felt as if I'd been hit on the head with a brick. My first thought was that she was having an affair. But she couldn't be. She wasn't like that. She was always so proper, disdaining unfaithfulness.

A few days before her departure, I did a scene in class from an experimental play called *The Beard* in which Billy the Kid and Jean Harlow end up together in hell. As Billy, I received rave reviews from my classmates and Milton Katselas. My performance was called everything from riveting to sexually erotic.

"You had every girl squirming in her seat," one of my classmates said.

Milton liked it so much he suggested I film the scene.

After class that night, Priscilla followed me out to my Jeep.

"I was so proud of you," she said.

She snuggled up to me and added, "You're the best actor in the class. I'm sorry I've been so tense and hard to get along with lately."

I knew that Priscilla had been feeling unsure about our relationship and I even suspected she was having an affair. But then she'd seen me do *The Beard* and Milton and the class had responded strongly to my work, and she had been so impressed herself that it had rekindled her passion for me.

That night she didn't have a headache, and the next day she informed me that there was an extra ticket for Tokyo if I wanted to come.

Tokyo made me temporarily forget about my suspicion that Priscilla was having an affair. One night after a concert we were drinking sake at a party, standing around the piano as Stevie Wonder sang and played for us. Soon most of the guests began singing along with Stevie, and I tried to get Priscilla to join in. She wouldn't, suddenly reverting to her aloof attitude.

"There are important industry people here," she snapped. "I think you should watch how much you drink."

"Everyone's drinking," I retorted.

"You don't have to."

When we returned to L.A., I told her that I knew there was something she wasn't telling me and we should have it out.

"We're both Scientologists," I said, "and we know that withholding things from each other is not okay."

She agreed. I went first, telling her about my affair in Florida with the photographer's assistant. I spared no details. Then I confessed about Manzanillo, editing out two of the three senoritas.

"Thank you for telling me," she said. "Is that all?"

For a moment I considered also talking to her about my growing feelings for Lisa. But I rationalized, saying to myself it was nothing and would go away as soon as Lisa got a boyfriend and that she was just a little more than thirteen years old and I couldn't possibly be interested in her.

"Yes," I said. "That's all I've done. Now it's your turn."

Priscilla braced herself.

"Michael, you have to promise you won't get angry with me."

As my stomach went to my throat, I realized that a fear I'd had since the day we'd started acting class was about to be confirmed.

"I've had an encounter," she said. "In class."

"Encounter? You mean you've slept with someone."

"You promised you wouldn't get angry."

"Who was it?"

When she told me it was her scene partner, I couldn't believe it.

"How could you make love to him? You said his breath stank something horrible!"

I knew I should sit there and listen, as she had when I'd spoken. Instead, I was so angry I got up and left the room. I stood out in the hall—I had to be by myself. I was afraid I was going to hit her. I wanted to grab hold of her and slam her into the wall and smash her little head to pieces. I kept seeing that actor's tongue slipping between her lips, the way it had the night they'd done their scene together in class. Why couldn't she at least have been more discreet, choosing a lover who wasn't in the same class and who I didn't have to face every day? She'd kicked me right in the balls, disgracing me in front of my peers. Now I knew exactly how Elvis had felt when he'd caught Priscilla having an affair right under his nose.

I scanned through my life, looking for a similar situation and how I'd handled it in the past. I remembered a girlfriend in New York who'd cheated on me, and after coaxing the details out of her by promising not to get upset, I'd thrown a bottle of wine against the wall and then smashed up the apartment. But that relationship hadn't been as important to me as this one was.

I was tempted to do the same thing to Priscilla and her house, but then a thought occurred to me. That's what Priscilla wanted. My head was pounding with crazy thoughts. Elvis should have shown her who the boss was the first time he caught her cheating on him. That would have straightened things out. Then he could have made mad, passionate love to her, and they could have made up, and they'd still be together. And he'd still be alive. But the poor bastard, addicted to drugs, had lost the ability to stand up like a man. He'd ended up alone. Maybe Priscilla was just too much of a woman for him.

I returned to the room, feeling in turmoil. We confessed a little more, and then we hugged. But I could feel a terrible strain between us and somehow I knew this was the beginning of the end. Power had changed hands, and I felt I'd lost control, handling her no better than Elvis. She had accepted my infidelities, but my rigid and stubborn ego wouldn't allow me to forgive hers. Instead, I wanted to punish her.

* * *

Shortly after that I did a scene in class from *Orpheus Descending.* Toward the end of the scene, as planned with my scene partner, I stripped myself naked. A gasp went up. It was my way of telling the class that I had bared my soul and trusted them and had been screwed. I never attended the class again. Nor did Priscilla.

Our relationship took on a different color and tone. Though the intimacy we'd shared when our love was virginal and hadn't yet been violated by betrayal was gone, we now seemed more relaxed with each other. I couldn't say for sure, but something about our recent troubles seemed to bring about a change in Priscilla. For one thing, she no longer took quite as many pains with her appearance. Before, she'd been a perfectionist when it came to clothes and makeup and hair. For another thing, surprisingly, she was now more aggressive sexually. Though different, the bond we now had was stronger than ever.

25

I enrolled in a different acting class and continued studying, still intent on an acting career. Except for television commercials, which I kept doing, including DIM lingerie for France, Presidente brandy for Mexico, and Chevrolet for the good old U.S.A., I'd given up modeling, and would only take an occasional print job if the money was too big to turn down. One night, returning from a shoot, I arrived home late. I'd been working since sunrise down at Laguna Beach. It had been one of those killer shootings with nearly fifty outfits to model in a single day in cold-assed weather —real energy-draining.

Upon entering the house, I heard Priscilla's cheerful greeting.

"If you go and take a hot shower," she said, "by the time you finish, I'll have dinner ready."

I couldn't remember ever hearing sweeter words. I gave Priscilla a little kiss, poured myself a glass of wine, and headed for the bedroom.

"Where's Lisa?" I hollered.

"She's spending the night with her girlfriend."

We had a leisurely dinner of Priscilla's homemade spaghetti with garlic bread and Caesar salad. She'd learned to make the spaghetti sauce from her mother, and I imagined Elvis had consumed gallons of it. It was excellent.

After dinner, Priscilla took my hand and spoke to me softly.

"Tonight I want to make love to you," she said. "You always make love to me. Tonight, it's my turn."

I could barely lift my wine glass to my mouth, I was so tired. Suddenly, I was wide awake and energized. She refilled our glasses, and I carried them to the bedroom.

Finishing in the bathroom before Priscilla, I waited patiently in bed for her to join me.

"Priscilla," I said. "I'm waiting. And I'm smiling."

I love it when a woman takes the initiative in lovemaking. There was a girl I'd lived with in Spain, and I always felt like she was in charge when we made love. She was so aggressive. Certain memories stay with you forever.

Priscilla called from her bathroom: "Turn out the lights."

"They're out," I said, quickly flicking the switch.

It was dark now, but I could see flickering candlelight through the beveled glass sections of her bathroom door. Women love candles. The softness of their illumination, contrasting with the violent shadows dancing on the ceiling and walls, represent to them, I've always believed, two undulating bodies in the act of love.

Priscilla came to the bed, holding her candle. She put it down on the nightstand. The candlelight revealed her full bosom under the sheer nightie, which came to just below her hips.

"What took you so long?" I teased. "Did you chicken out?"

"Lay back and put your arms above your head and shut up."

Holding my wrists, keeping me down, she moved slowly on top of me, and I gazed up at our reflection in the mirror over the bed. Her naked hips had an exquisite white bikini line across them.

When an extremely feminine and beautiful lady skips the usual tenderness of foreplay and takes on the dominant role of the male, it's overwhelming. I let her enjoy me for a long time, until I sensed my control going. Our mouths deliciously meshed together as one. I took her buttocks firmly, and, in one quick move, I pulled her in to me and rolled over, taking charge.

"Don't move until you feel me throb inside you," I said. "Then do the same back to me from inside yourself."

We began a slow, tantalizing rhythm, and what I was showing her was the joy of orgasm without movement. I used my strength to keep either of us from moving an inch, to prolong that moment of no return.

Feeling our bodies trembling uncontrollably, I sensed the time was right and said, "Now, Priscilla. Let yourself go now."

We climaxed together. It felt as if we would never stop. A peaceful stillness enveloped us, and we lay in silence.

"I've missed you, Michael," she said. "I haven't felt like this with you in a long time."

"I've missed you, too, Priscilla."

"I don't want to lose us, Michael. We've come too far now."

Feeling me beginning to grow again inside her, she asked, "How can you be getting turned on again?"

"It always happens like that when I'm raped, like I just was."

We made love again, and afterward, when we were falling asleep, we clasped hands, and Priscilla nestled her head on my chest.

"I wish I could love as deeply as you do, from the heart," I said.

"You do, Michael. You have with me. I've felt it. You're just afraid to admit it. You don't give yourself enough credit. You're a good man—a very generous person. I've never known anyone as wonderful as you."

"I don't think I am, baby. Sometimes I feel like I don't even deserve to have you."

"You're a good dad to Caroline, and the best actor I've ever seen in my life. I mean that. If you stay as dedicated as you are, you'll get recognition soon."

"Baby, it means a lot to me when you tell me that. I get so doubtful sometimes. I think that's why I'm always trying to act so tough, like things don't bother me."

"It's okay to feel that way. We all do sometimes. I don't know what I'd do if I didn't have you to come home to."

"You're just saying that."

"No one takes care of things like you do, and I know everything will be all right as long as you're there."

We fell asleep, and when I woke up later, Priscilla's head was still on my chest. Looking outside through the French doors, I could see the full moon. The doors were open, and there was a chill in the crisp early morning air. I reached outside the cover and rubbed Willy's head. He moaned happily and sat up, stretching groggily. He sniffed my hand and licked it. Then he went outside through the doggie door.

I looked down at Priscilla's sleeping face. Any other man

would have been happy, I thought. But I wasn't, and something was tearing me up. Some part of me had always remained a small boy with the childhood expectations that my mother had instilled in me—be your own person. Grandma had always said, "Mike has a conscience. He'll never go wrong for too long. When he does something he's not proud of, it will weigh on him. He can't live with that, and eventually he'll always make it right."

I felt like half a man, living in Priscilla's house. I wanted us living in a place I provided. I had been raised to believe that the man is the provider. I didn't feel I was doing that, and it made me feel as if I weren't being true to myself. It would eventually be our undoing, unless I did something about it.

26

It was 1981, and we were in our third year together; there was now a sense of maturity in our relationship.

But as usual, when you don't want something, it comes at you in abundance. Major modeling jobs were being offered me weekly. I didn't want to be separated from Priscilla, nor did I want to leave my new acting class. I'd just signed with a theatrical agent, and I was already up for a role in *Mommie Dearest*.

When Yves Saint-Laurent made me an offer I just couldn't turn down, I accepted a lucrative trip to New York City. At the same time, Priscilla was preparing to leave for a music festival in Vina del Mar, Chile, as one of Julio Iglesias's invited guests.

"Michael, come with me," Priscilla pleaded. "You and I could have a wonderful time. We've never been to South America together."

It would mean canceling my New York trip, and I wouldn't be able to make the final callback for *Mommie Dearest* either. By now I'd heard that Faye Dunaway was going to be in this film. It was sounding more and more provocative to me. I had to stay and focus on my new career if I was ever going to make a serious attempt at acting. I assured Priscilla that while she was away we'd talk on the phone every night.

"Don't worry about us," I said. "We're doing fine now. When I lived in Spain, I really loved Julio's music, and you're in for a real treat."

I was in New York for three days before Priscilla and I spoke again. I had been trying constantly to reach her in Vina del Mar by long-distance with no success, leaving my number and messages at her hotel. With the time difference, it was almost impossible to make contact.

I was staying with Joe Hunter, the head agent at Ford's, who had a town house on Park Avenue. Also staying there as Joe's houseguest was a well-endowed, long-stemmed beauty, another top model. We had an intimate conversation, alone at Joe's, with me sitting on the edge of her bed. She looked gorgeous, and I told her so. I also told her I was in a very precarious place in my relationship with Priscilla, but under any other circumstances, I would be very attracted to her.

On my last day in New York, Priscilla finally reached me at the studio where I was shooting.

"Michael, you were right about Julio. He's wonderful. I've shown him your pictures and told him all about you."

"What pictures?"

"You know, the ones I carry of you in my wallet."

"What did you show them to him for?"

"He asked all kinds of questions about you, and I just showed them to him. I'm proud of you."

I began to worry. It had never occurred to me that she'd fall for him. I knew he'd been married and was the father of children, so I didn't think of him as a threat. I'd always thought of him as an older Frank Sinatra type, harmless and balding.

Maybe he wasn't so old and balding, after all. And he was a Latin.

"He wants to meet you when he comes to L.A.," Priscilla said. "And he also invited me to come with him to Brazil for the rest of the festival."

"Are you going?"

"I'd love to, if you don't mind. I'm having so much fun."

If I didn't mind? What was she, crazy? Thinking I'd let her run after the world's most famous Latin lover! There they'd be—standing in Rio on top of Sugar Loaf Mountain, Julio charming Priscilla with, "who can hold back what is written on the wind?"

"He's a gentleman," Priscilla added. "Just like you."

If she thought she was reassuring me by calling Julio a gentleman like me, she was nuts. Women had always told me that it was my gentlemanly ways they'd fallen for.

"He has that same magic Elvis had," she said. "I told him he should come to the States. But he's very insecure about that. His English isn't very good."

The photographer's assistant tugged my sleeve and said, "Michael, we're ready for you."

I told Priscilla I had to go. I was catching a late flight back to L.A. that night, and I'd talk to her the next day.

As I was about to hang up, she said, "If you don't want me to go, I won't. But I'm having fun, Michael."

"I'll call you tomorrow."

The following evening, back in L.A., I tried calling her for hours. When she finally answered, she was excited and breathless.

"I was just getting ready to call you!" she said.

"It's late," I pointed out. "I've been trying to reach you all night."

"We just finished dinner."

"It's three in the morning down there, Priscilla."

"They eat late here. And then Julio pleaded with me to stay with him for the last show. He's nervous about this new young Latin star who's on the rise. I just came back to my room to freshen up."

"You mean you're going back out again?"

"Yes. Julio's waiting in the limo."

"I don't believe this. I've got to be up for a 5:00 A.M. call, and you're spending the night out with another guy."

"Did you get that part in *Mommie Dearest?*"

"You don't give a damn."

"Michael, have you been drinking?"

"You'd be drinking, too, if you felt like I do."

"You're being ridiculous. There's nothing between Julio and me. And please don't drink. Your eyes puff up when you do."

"Oh, fuck that! Just go run off with Julio!"

Priscilla put her manager on the line.

"I thought you were supposed to be taking care of her," I said. "You're her manager, and you're all down there partying all night long."

"It's good for her career to be here," he said. "Don't get crazy."

We got into a shouting match, yelling obscenities at each other.

"Put Priscilla back on the phone," I demanded. "This is none of you business."

"She's already gone," he said.

I slammed the phone down. How dare she turn our private fight over to a manager? He had no business interfering with us. I looked around the bedroom, jerked open the night-table drawer, and grabbed the .38 I kept in there. It was loaded and ready to use. I pointed it at the large painting above the fireplace. It showed two girls, one seated, the other standing behind her, and this painting had always reminded me of Priscilla and her sister—the queen and her lady-in-waiting. I wanted to blow it to pieces.

There was a knock on the door.

"Merkly," Lisa called, "what are you yelling about?"

I put the gun away and told Lisa to come in.

"I could hear you yelling all the way down in my room," she said.

"I'm sorry if I woke you. I just had a fight with your mother, and I don't know what to do. I think I'm losing her."

Lisa came over and sat down on the bed beside me, patting my knee.

"Mommy won't ever leave you."

"I don't know about that."

"I know she won't."

I looked up at Lisa, who was now thirteen, and she had never looked more appealing to me. For a moment, I wanted to take her into my arms and love her right there in the bed that her mother and I shared. As if reading my mind, Lisa rose, leaned down and kissed me on the cheek, and said, grinning, "Go to bed now, Merkly. Don't be so upset with my mother."

After she left, I went outside. I felt like I was suffocating. Willy followed behind me, and for a while I sat by the pool with my dog, listening to the coyotes yapping somewhere in the canyons. Then I went down to the tennis court, the tall stadium lights looming up into the darkness. An owl that I'd always seen around the grounds was perched on top of one of the big fixtures, looking down and checking me out. I clapped my hands sharply and he flew off toward Pickfair. Willy nudged my hand with his wet nose; he had a tennis ball in his mouth and wanted me to throw it for him. We played a long time that night.

I guess Priscilla was trying to tell me, in her own way, that she had finally found freedom from Elvis and was now beginning to enjoy, once again, all the things she'd left behind as a young girl. Could I blame her for that?

27

I didn't sleep very much that night, tossing and turning, thinking about Priscilla down in Chile with Julio. After Willy and I played his game of tennis, I finally went to bed around 3:30 A.M.

I reported to makeup at Paramount at six o'clock for my role as Ted Gelber, Joan Crawford's lover. The makeup man was concerned about the puffiness underneath my eyes and handed me two cotton balls soaked in witch hazel.

"Sit down over there and hold these over your eyes for a while. It'll take the swelling out."

Sitting there, I started thinking about Priscilla again. Frank Perry poked his head in the door.

"Everybody okay?" he asked.

I nodded yes.

Seeing my condition, he said, "What's wrong, Michael?"

"He's just having a little early morning snooze," the makeup man said.

"Would you like some coffee?" Frank asked.

I told him no thanks, I'd already had some. He put his hand on my shoulder.

"When you're ready," he said, "I'd like you to come over and meet Faye. We can run over your lines together before we start shooting."

I was thankful I had a director who cared about me and treated me with respect.

"Do you have any further questions about playing Ted Gelber?" Frank asked.

"No," I said. "Not really. I'm living a similar story at home."

Frank made me feel comfortable, and I momentarily forgot about what was going on down in South America with the woman I loved. After he introduced me to Faye Dunaway and ran us through our scene, Frank got behind the camera and started filming.

I lay down next to Faye Dunaway on the love seat. Pushing her hair away from her neck, I kissed her there softly. Faye's head went back in rapture. She raised her leg and rolled over close to me. I reached for her, my hand sliding up the inside of her thigh. I could feel the warm, silky skin above her stocking. I stopped kissing her neck and tenderly brushed my lips across her cheek, pausing at her mouth. We lay there breathing in each other. There was a scent of lavender and lipstick about her.

Out of the corner of my eye, I saw someone in the doorway. Mara Hobel, the girl playing Joan Crawford's daughter, was standing there, looking at us and holding a glass of vodka.

"We've got company," I said.

Faye pulled away and sat up, straightening her stockings and smoothing her hair. Then she glared at Mara.

"Cut!" Frank Perry called. "That's a print!"

The normal commotion resumed on the set, and Faye said to me, "Was it as good as when we rehearsed?"

"It was excellent, Faye."

"Are you sure?"

"It was so quiet in here, you could hear a pin drop. I don't think anyone was even breathing, except you and me."

I couldn't believe Faye Dunaway was asking me for reassurance, but that's how she was in real life. It was clear to me why she was a superstar—she personified vulnerability, warmth, and womanliness. She couldn't have been more lovable.

My successful work on *Mommie Dearest* helped me forget my jealousy over Julio, and when Priscilla returned I told her I was sorry for the way I'd spoken to her on the phone and for jumping to conclusions. She told me she'd turned down Julio's insistent invitations and hadn't flown on with him to Rio.

"It was my fault," I said. "I couldn't control my anger. With you being so far away, I felt as if I had no way to fight for you."

"He was just a real friend to me, Michael. I really liked him, but that's all it was."

Priscilla and I started spending our weekends in Palm Springs, and we finally decided to get a hideaway there. We chose a secluded area, Desert Hot Springs, which had excellent security. Lisa had just turned fourteen, and Priscilla wanted a place where Lisa could safely have guests come with us on the weekends. Lisa was unhappy not having anyone her age to have fun with when the three of us went away.

Palm Springs became a favorite place of Lisa's, because Priscilla finally consented to letting her bring her boyfriend. He'd have to sleep on the couch in the living room, she said, but Lisa was in heaven. She and her boyfriend took long walks in the evening, and they ended up sneaking into the neighbor's Jacuzzi.

Priscilla was always acting like a house mother, and after fifteen or twenty minutes of Lisa being gone with her boyfriend, she'd go out and call to her to come home. One evening, Priscilla came in rather pale in the face, telling me, "I caught them next door in the Jacuzzi!"

"What were they doing?" I asked, smiling. I loved always teasing Priscilla.

"Michael, I can't let her out of my sight for a minute. I don't know why she has to be like that. She's boy crazy."

"She takes after you, baby," I said.

"Michael, it's not funny."

"Priscilla, when did you last see her this happy? She's smiling all the time. She pitches in without being asked, and I couldn't believe it when she set the table the other night on her own. I'm happy for her. And I like her boyfriend."

Priscilla's sister had come to Palm Springs with us for the weekend and had taken Lisa and her boyfriend to the movies. I told Priscilla to go into the kitchen and get the bottle of Dom Perignon that I'd put in the freezer.

"Bring it to the bathroom," I said. "Let's take a bath together."

I filled the bathtub until it was steaming and overflowing with bubbles. Climbing into the tub and sliding down into the water, I mused over Priscilla catching Lisa and her boyfriend and remembered the first time I'd been caught by my grandfather while masturbating. It was so embarrassing. I'd pretended I had a terrible itch, and Grandpa had just smiled and said, "Be careful or that'll turn you to stone."

Priscilla came into the bathroom carrying the champagne in one hand and a corkscrew in the other.

"You don't need a corkscrew to open champagne," I told her.

"I've never opened a bottle myself," she said.

"Didn't you and Elvis ever have champagne?"

"Yes, but someone else always opened it for us."

I popped open the bottle, poured us each a glass, and watched Priscilla as she undressed. She was trying to be sexy for me, but she was so modest that she kept holding a towel in front of her. I grabbed the towel and pulled her toward me. We curled up in the tub together and toasted each other.

"If you could just believe how much I love you, Michael."

I looked at her and grinned. "I'll believe it if you do me a favor. Turn on the radio."

"I got the champagne. You handle the music."

I got out of the tub, trying not to flood the bathroom, and turned on the stereo.

"You have such a cute little butt," she said. "Just like a football player's—all small and tight."

As I got back into the tub, I said, "Did you and Elvis ever do this?"

"No, or I'd have known how to open the champagne bottle."

"What was the craziest thing you ever did sexually? I

masturbated inside a cement mixer once. I had a job in high school, chipping the concrete out, and got bored."

"I guess it was when Elvis had me wear panties and wrestle around on the bed with that girl while he filmed us."

"I bet he masturbated, watching the film later?"

"I don't think so. But I know when Mr. Presley got mad at him, he'd tell Elvis, 'You're not good for anything but pulling your peter.'"

"Most guys love to do that. I bet you wish you had one."

"I've often thought it would be cute to be able to stand up and go to the bathroom in the snow."

"What'd you really do with that girl?"

"We just hugged and rolled around on the bed for Elvis."

"He didn't want you to do anything else?"

"No."

I touched Priscilla very lovingly, the way I imagined a girl might do it.

"She didn't do this to you?"

"This is turning you on, isn't it, Michael?"

"Thinking of you and that girl in bed is very much of a turn-on."

"I can see that."

We'd been fondling each other in the warm bath water. I pulled Priscilla close to me, taking her hand in mine.

"We've been through some pretty tough times," I said. "Some of them I even thought had destroyed us. But you always seemed to understand—always tried so damn hard to make us work out."

"I wish Elvis and I could have talked like this."

"You never did?"

"Yes, earlier, but then his drugs became more important to him."

"How come that happened?"

"Studios were sending him the most ridiculous scripts to do. After a while he'd say, 'I don't have to even read them. They're all alike. Why won't they send me something better to do, just once?' "

"They were only interested in making money off him," I said.

"Elvis was terribly frustrated by his movie career. He even became physically ill from some of the scenes he had to do."

"Why'd he keep doing them? Why didn't he stop?"

"He had a contract with MGM that paid him to do what they said. Anyway, he needed the money. He spent a lot, on everything, all the time."

"It sounds like he was allowing people to not only tell him what to do in his career but also in his personal life."

"He'd become so lost, he didn't know who to turn to anymore."

"It's incredible how we can let ourselves get so messed up."

"I don't want that to ever happen to us, Michael."

"It won't."

"I love you, Michael. We're lucky with what we have."

For a man who was used to getting his own way, Elvis must have felt exasperated, mass-producing all those fluff movies, having to act like a wind-up doll, letting the studios dress him up any way they wanted and doing their bidding. He'd frolic, jump, kiss girls, zoom fast in sporty cars, dance the cha-cha, waterski, do the hula and be a frogman. I understood why he'd got hooked on so many drugs. No man could be proud of himself who was only creating meaningless fluff. I'd felt the same way on many occasions modeling clothes, just like a dress-up doll.

28

It was the rainy season in Southern California. For two months there'd been torrential downpours, and mud slides were threatening homes throughout the canyons of Bel Air and Beverly Hills. Priscilla and I took the Mercedes and headed for Palm Springs. She had some Presley estate business to take care of there. Graceland Enterprises was putting Elvis's Palm Springs house up for sale, and she needed to inventory his personal effects, decide what she wanted to keep for herself and what was to be shipped back to Graceland. Nothing could be left, because souvenir-hunters would pick the place clean.

When we arrived the air inside the house was musty and smoky, and the carpets were one solid stain. It looked like nothing had been changed since Elvis's death years ago. I found it unbelievable that someone had let the house sit here empty for so long.

"When they had parties," Priscilla explained, "the guys could get pretty sloppy."

"Did you come here with him often?"

"Not so often. He liked this place as a retreat for himself."

I bet he did, I thought. This house and the entertainment that went on in it were what caused the final crumbling of their marriage.

"Who was taking care of Elvis when he died?" I asked.

"I don't know. Probably the girlfriend who was living with him."

"From the looks of this place, an unhappy, lonely person lived here. Someone who'd given up and just didn't care anymore."

We walked from room to room, opening cabinets and closets. In the kitchen, a can opener still lay on the counter. The cabinets were full of canned goods, and the refrigerator had frozen vegetables in the freezer that had become one solid chunk of ice.

I took some cans of Vienna sausages and pork and beans from the cabinet.

"Did Elvis eat this kind of stuff?" I asked.

"The guys didn't care what they ate when they were by themselves," Priscilla said, walking away and leaving me in the kitchen.

I looked at his dishes, taking a stack of them down from the shelf. They were plastic and mismatched, some cream-colored and others with little green leaves printed around the rims, the kind you buy at Woolworth's. I thought it strange that the King would have such cheap stuff. I suppose I expected fancy china. I put everything back and closed the cabinet door. Seeing these remains of a life that had fallen completely apart made me sad.

I joined Priscilla in the den, where she was sitting at a large synthesizer and going through stacks of papers and sheet music. Marginal notes were scribbled on the music. I wanted to read them but couldn't make out the handwriting.

We walked outside to the swimming pool. Old, wrought-iron lawn furniture stood about, and there was a cracked frisbee sitting in the corner where it had last landed, next to a child's rubber beach ball. The barbecue grill looked like it had been used a million times and never cleaned. The potted plants resembled burned stubs. It was late and we could see the lights beginning to blink on in the desert city below.

I followed Priscilla to the recreation room. There was a gigantic video screen, a pool table, and a jukebox filled with records. I sat down on a giant, sectional, brown suede couch and Priscilla said, "That was Elvis's place. He'd sit there with the guys and their girlfriends, and they'd watch movies all night long."

"Does this upset you, being here again?" I asked.

"It brings back memories. I remember when the alarm system was installed. Elvis wanted laser beams that would trip off the alarm if someone walked through a room. He also had the entire floor wired."

"Sounds like he was paranoid," I said.

"Michael, you'd never believe how people behaved, trying to get to him. They'd do anything. He needed a place like this to feel safe. Although I don't think he'd have heard the alarm if it had gone off."

We went into Elvis's bedroom. There was a big oversized bed with a blue spread and matching sheets, and the carpet was powder blue. Priscilla had been calm until now, but suddenly she looked disturbed. There were stains on the carpet and the bed. They reminded me of body fluids. She walked over to the blackout curtains and pulled them aside, but it was dark outside.

I went into Elvis's bathroom to let her be alone with her thoughts. Looking inside the medicine cabinet, I saw a bottle of Brut, several blue disposable razors, a well-squeezed tube of Colgate, Edge shaving cream, a couple of used syringes, and a stack of small bars of motel soap. I opened the Brut and patted some on my face. I'd never liked the smell before. It was always too sweet for me, but now it smelled good. Closing the cabinet, I looked in the mirror and expected to see him standing beside me.

We would have to take all of these things and dispose of them.

I slid open the glass shower door and picked up a dried, stiff, wrung-out washcloth and smelled it.

"Michael," Priscilla said.

I turned and saw her standing in the doorway, visibly disturbed.

"I want to leave," she said.

I felt awkward, standing there with Elvis's petrified washcloth in my hand. What was I doing, going through her ex-husband's things? I didn't belong here, and suddenly felt this was no place for me.

I put my arm around her and led her out.

"I'll have my sister drive up from L.A. later in the week and take care of the rest of this," she said.

Before we left, I picked up a stuffed owl of Elvis's and a lighted globe of the world.

"This owl would look great in our bedroom, above the grandfather clock," I said. "And I think Lisa might like this illuminated globe. Should we take them now?"

"If you want to," Priscilla said. "And then let's leave."

We walked outside and Priscilla climbed into the car immediately, not waiting, as she usually did, for me to open the door for her.

I turned to take one last look at the house, silhouetted against the mountains, and I could have sworn I heard the faint sounds of singing, excited voices, guitars, and Elvis's laughter.

We stopped at our favorite Italian restaurant in Palm Springs, drinking heavy red wine to get rid of our melancholy feelings. After dinner, on the way back to L.A. in the 280SL convertible that had once belonged to Elvis, Priscilla leaned her head out as we sped along the highway, letting the warm desert air blow her hair.

"I love these hot desert nights," she said.

"What really happened between you two?" I asked. "You and Elvis had everything."

"I grew up," she said, quietly. After a moment, she added, "He was never satisfied. And he was tired of singing. He wanted to be doing something more than singing rock 'n' roll at fifty. His age was really beginning to scare him."

"No one's ever satisfied with what they have," I said. "We always want something more."

"I don't think you could ever be satisfied with just one woman," Priscilla said. "You've been around too many beautiful models. When we go to bed, I sometimes wonder why you're with me when you've been with all of them. At first, I used to always look in your closet when you'd go away on a trip, to see if you took all your clothes with you. I was so worried you weren't coming back."

"How could you be so insecure, baby? You could have any man you want."

"I've known those rich, powerful men."

"You mean there was someone richer than Elvis?"

"He could have bought and sold Elvis many times over."

"Why didn't you marry him?"

"Because to him a woman was just another possession."

"That reminds me of a rich, older woman I dated once."

"Who was she?"

I told her about Merle Oberon and me. Priscilla and I had been through so much by now I didn't think it would hurt her.

I'd just arrived in California, and I was broke. A guy I'd met at a party in Malibu introduced us. It was lust at first sight. Merle used to invite me down to Acapulco all the time. She had a villa there known as the Taj Mahal of Mexico. She was married to a rich Italian industrialist who had his own estate in Mexico City. She'd have me picked up at the airport in an old black Ford sedan. She referred to it as her South of the Border Limo.

There were always guests like Noel Coward and Luis Estevez around Merle's villa, but I'd show up in cutoffs, long hair, and stoned on Mexican grass. After dinner each evening, when everyone had turned in, she'd give me a signal to come to her room. The signal was a little light at the far end of the hallway. I'd have to sneak around behind the main part of the house, through the bougainvillea, tap on a side window, and wait for the little light to go out. That meant she was ready for me. I remember that first night. As I got ready to climb in her bed, she said, "Just a minute. Did you wash your feet?"

I said, "You mean, since I just got here?"

"Yes."

"No," I said. "I haven't."

"Would you mind going in the bathroom and washing them?"

I washed them for her, even though they were clean. I'd only walked through wet grass, coming from my room. I chuckled as I washed my feet in her bidet.

Priscilla thoroughly enjoyed my story, but said, "Wasn't Merle Oberon quite a bit older than you?"

"She sure was. She was making movies in the forties. But her body was still firm. Her hips and breasts were so firm I couldn't believe it. What happened to you and the rich guy you were with?"

"I met him in Vegas when Elvis was playing the International. He owned some hotels and casinos, as well as a movie studio. He was always a gentleman and never asked me out until after Elvis and I were separated. I went to London and St. Tropez with him and stayed on his yacht. Like your affair, ours was also discreet. He'd have me wait until everyone went to bed and then call me and ask if I'd like to come to his room."

"How old was he?"

"He had kids about my age."

"How could he still get it up?"

"He kept in excellent shape and took pride in his physique, always exercising, like you. But I sometimes felt like I was just something for him to amuse himself with."

"I began to feel like that with Merle, too. Then, Luis, who'd introduced us, told me that Merle had grown very fond of me. About that time my modeling career took off, and we didn't see each other as often. Not too long afterward, she divorced her husband and married a young man my age."

"Do you ever wish you'd stayed with her?"

"I often considered it. She was very dear to me, and one of the kindest persons I've ever known. There was something natural about her, and even with all her wealth she still had a simplicity. I felt we had something special. When we made love, there was a gentleness. We were similar in many ways."

"Were you in love with her?"

"In a way. I remember our long, elegant lunches in the sun, and swimming all day together. She introduced me to her son and daughter, and I taught them how to swim."

"The man I was seeing wanted to get serious, too. But I didn't want to be controlled again. I'd had enough of that with Elvis."

Though I was driving, I pulled Priscilla over next to me, practically in my lap.

"I'm glad that guy was too old for you," I said, taking her hand and putting it down on me. "But I'm not too old for you."

"Michael," she protested. "You're terrible! Why are you so turned on?"

"Because I've been dreaming about something I want you to do."

She grinned and looked at me out of the corner of her eye.

29

Ever since that afternoon I'd photographed Lisa, my affection for her had grown to the point that it became an issue in my relationship with Priscilla. Once, when Priscilla and I were sitting at the dinner table and Lisa was sitting between us, Lisa got up to get something from the refrigerator and her bare knee accidently brushed against my hand. It sent waves of desire through me. I looked at Priscilla and thought, Can't you see what's happening— I've fallen in love with your daughter.

Lisa was reaching womanhood, and now, when we walked on the street, men turned around and looked back at her. She'd developed curves all over and with her sandy blond hair and milky complexion, she was quite a sight.

I was with Lisa constantly—after school and in the evenings when her mother was working. I'd had to put an end to our swimming together after one disturbing afternoon in the pool. Lisa had innocently thrown her arms around me, and we were jumping up and down. When we got into deeper water and her feet couldn't touch the bottom, she wrapped her legs around me, and we continued playfully bouncing up and down. I became aroused.

A sick feeling crept slowly into the pit of my stomach. I was craving Lisa sexually. I tickled her and pushed her away and told her to go take a shower and we'd get dinner ready for her mother. I watched her glistening wet body as she ran up the steps, past the garden, and disappeared inside the house.

Everything was out of control, and I realized I had to get away from all this—the house, Lisa, and even Priscilla.

One night not long after, Priscilla and I returned home after having a horrendous argument over my drinking and her getting roses from Julio. She went into her bathroom, and I went to Lisa's room.

I wanted someone to talk to, but Lisa was asleep. I lifted a corner of the covers and gazed at her. She was lying on her back, and her honey-colored hair was spread out over the pillow. She was my beloved, and I couldn't even tell her.

The next morning I woke up with a hangover, alone in bed. I opened my eyes and saw Priscilla and Lisa sitting on the white embroidered sofa at the foot of the bed. They were both grinning, and I caught the end of their conversation. It was something to do with Elvis, and Lisa was saying, "Bless his sick little ol' self."

"What's going on?" I asked.

"Why did you go to Lisa's room last night?"

"I wanted to talk to her," I said.

"What about?"

"You and I had argued so much, I needed someone to talk to."

Priscilla looked at Lisa and said, "Lisa, do you have any questions?"

"Yeah," Lisa said. "Why did you lift up the sheets?"

I wanted to pour my heart out to Lisa and beg Priscilla to understand. I cared so much for Lisa. The feelings I had for her I knew I would never have for another. Everything about her was exactly what I wanted in a woman.

"I just wanted to see you, Lisa" I said. "I'm really sorry if I scared you, and you have my word it won't happen again." Everything seemed okay after that, but a short time later Priscilla told me that she didn't feel it was a good idea for Lisa and me to be alone in the house. She asked me to explain what there was between Lisa and me. I wanted to tell her I was in love with Lisa, but how do you tell the woman you're in love with that you're also in love with her daughter? I realized this was one thing I couldn't discuss with Priscilla.

I was slipping off the edge, losing a grip on my sanity. I couldn't think clearly any more. My feelings for Lisa were so strong I realized I needed to get away from her before I went nuts.

It was time for a separation. Priscilla and I talked, and by mutual consent, I moved out. We called it "giving ourselves some space," but what it really amounted to was an attempt to break up.

On many occasions, I'd wanted to get away by myself for a while, to try to find some emotional stability, but the only place I owned was a condo in Colorado. I decided to sell it and I bought a place in L.A., just north of Sunset Boulevard in the Sunset Plaza area. It was a Mediterranean-style building with white iron balconies, striped awnings, and palm trees around the pool. It stood on a hill overlooking the flats of Hollywood, and you could see all the way across La Cienaga Pass to the Pacific Ocean. I would make my new home there.

30

<hr/>

After our separation, at first I enjoyed the freedom to come and go as I pleased. I revisited my former haunts, revived lost friendships, and met new girls. But the late nights began to show on my face, and my film career, promising since *Mommie Dearest*, was promising no more. On one interview, I overheard a secretary remark, as I was leaving the producer's office, "That can't be him. He looks terrible!" Despite my somewhat worn looks, though, my modeling career kept going strong.

I couldn't get Priscilla out of my mind. We saw each other occasionally but she was caught up in her rising star, doing PR layouts, talk shows, and personal appearances.

Then one day she invited me to Trump's for tea, saying she had some exciting news. After we were shown to a cozy little table in the rear, she studied me a moment and said, "You're not taking care of yourself."

"I'm fine," I said. "Tell me your news!"

As she poured my tea, her blouse opened slightly in the front, and I could see the little lacy fringes of her bra.

"I have my first movie," she said. "It's not the lead, but it's a good role. I'm leaving for Thailand in about three weeks."

My heart sank, but I said, "That's wonderful. Who else is in it?"

"Michael Landon and Jergen Procknow, of *Das Boot*. Jergen's a German star."

I could already see the headlines: "Priscilla Falls in Love in Bangkok."

"What kind of role is it?" I asked.

She told me the story. It took place after the Vietnam war, and Michael Landon would be playing a real-life journalist who had to swim underwater across the Mekong River for a dangerous rescue of his girlfriend, who was being held captive in Laos. Priscilla was to play a beautiful young woman who teaches Landon how to scuba dive.

"I'm so nervous," she said. "I've never scuba dived except for that time with you in Mexico."

Over the years, I'd spent a lot of time teaching her how to swim.

"You're a good swimmer," I reminded her. "You'll learn scuba quickly."

"I hope so. I've hired a private instructor from the Y."

"Then there's nothing to worry about."

"There's something else. I have to do a dive from the high board."

"You mean the three-meter board?"

She nodded.

"A crash course in scuba is one thing, baby," I cautioned, "but trying to learn how to dive in a few days is madness, especially off the three-meter board. It still makes me nervous, and I've had years of diving experience."

"Don't frighten me! I've already started at UCLA with one of the women coaches out there."

"How's it going?"

"She just sits on the edge of the pool telling me what to do. She won't even get wet."

"Has she put you on the high board yet?"

"No. She still has me jumping off the low board. I want to do my own stunt work more than anything I've ever wanted in my life."

"You want me to help you?"

"No, that's okay."

"Don't be so damned stubborn. You know there's nobody else who can teach you something that tough."

"I know, but I didn't want to bother you."

"I've spent half my life on diving boards, and you're crazy if you think I'm going to stand by while you break your neck."

After that, we met daily at the Sunset Canyon "Rec" Center, where the UCLA dive team trains.

I knew I'd have to push her beyond any limit she'd ever imagined. I told her I'd be tough with her and show her no mercy. She told me she trusted me and knew I would make her "get it."

I had to make her more afraid of me than the high board. I would have to terrify her, just as my boot camp drill instructors had done to me at seventeen. She would learn to dive safely and she would gain a new courage, even though I suspected that it would also cause her to hate me. Under normal conditions I teach slowly, with love, but we only had two weeks for her to learn something that requires months.

The first time she climbed on the board she got halfway to the end, broke down in tears, and retreated, crawling back to the ladder. I climbed up and told her she was facing the biggest hurdle of her life. Walking out on the board, I did the dive for her, a jackknife.

A few minutes later, climbing back up the ladder, I said, "I still get butterflies myself, Priscilla. It's all part of it."

"I feel better now. You make it look so easy."

By the end of the day, I had her jumping feet first off the high board.

The next day I had her sit at the end of the board, put her hands in front of her, between her legs, and look down.

"Just rock forward and go in," I said.

Her fear overtook her again.

"Michael, it's too high. I'm afraid I'll hurt my face."

She again crawled back to the ladder, and this time, she was crying.

"Don't be a quitter!" I said.

"I'm not a quitter! I'm afraid."

"Do it for yourself, Priscilla."

But she was already halfway down the ladder. She grabbed her towel and stalked off. I went after her, took her by the shoulder and spun her around. I hated myself for what I was about to say but knew I had to get her angry enough to make her forget her fear of diving.

"You're acting like a coward. You fake a real big game, don't you? Saying, I'm Priscilla Presley! Well, big deal! You're nothing without Elvis. You can't even get on a diving board by yourself and do a little dive. I thought you had more guts."

"I'm going to let a stunt woman do it. I never wanted to do it anyway."

I grabbed her by the wrist and dragged her back to the board.

"You're going to get your ass up there before I kick it,

and you're going to do the damn dive or I'll carry you up there myself and throw you off the end."

"I'll scream for the lifeguard—!"

I reached down to pick her up and she realized I meant business.

"Put me down! You're embarrassing me. I'll do it, damn you!"

"Get up there, now!"

"Let me catch my breath—just for a minute!"

I reached for her again and she scooted up the ladder.

"I hate you!" she called, looking back down at me. "After I do this, I'm leaving the pool and I never want to see you again."

"Good! Get up there and sit on the end of the board."

She walked sobbing to the end of the board and sat down.

I followed, and stood behind her.

"What do I do now?"

"Put your arms out straight in front of you. Left hand over right hand. Thumbs interlocked. Rock back. When I say, go, rock forward and look for the water."

I said, "Go!" As she rocked forward, I pushed her lightly, helping her go over, and she sailed through the air, entering the water smoothly.

Her head popped to the surface. She wasn't actually grinning, but I could see a new respect in her eyes.

"I did it!" she said.

"It's just the beginning," I said, growling like a DI. Then I smiled and said, "You're going to be a hell of a diver."

I coached her for the two weeks. Her confidence grew, and soon I had her standing up on the board. I taught her the approach, and eventually got her to spring off the board. On the day before she left for Thailand, she successfully executed the dive.

Meanwhile, my own affairs suffered. I'd put everything aside to work with Priscilla, canceling my acting interviews, showing up late or unprepared, and I was neglecting modeling altogether. Every time I was alone, I kept hearing the same questions in my head, Do I really have love for this woman? Is she worth what I'm doing to my life? I always received the same answers: yes, I do, and yes, she is. I'd been hoping that the coaching would bring us together again. I wanted Priscilla to feel the same way and ask me to come to Bangkok. She didn't.

She was on her way to Asia—the other side of the world. Through her secretary, she sent me a letter that she'd written at the airport. I again hoped it would be an invitation. But it wasn't.

In the letter, she wrote how nervous she was about going to a foreign country for her first picture and how much she missed me and how dedicated I'd been in teaching her. She said she viewed me as a professional and had felt, during our work, that she absolutely had to "get it." She thanked me for my time and devotion and love and added that I was special to her and that she'd be thinking of me. She told me to work hard on my own career, because I was talented and soon it would be my turn.

The final boarding announcement was being called, she wrote, and she wished the severe pain in her neck from her nervous condition would go away. She ended the letter by repeating that she loved me.

31

Before Priscilla left for Bangkok we went to see *Das Boot*, wanting to check out her costar Jergen Procknow. I hoped he'd be buck-toothed and crosseyed, but no such luck. He was striking, sensitive, and a powerful actor—and I hated him.

"He's so good," she said.

She took my hand and asked if she could sit in my lap. I let her, and even though my legs went to sleep, I knew she needed as much reassurance as I could give her, and I continued to hold her. She stayed curled up on me through half the movie.

About a week later, after she reported to work in Thailand, she called me from Chieng Mai.

"How's the movie going?" I asked.

"I haven't worked yet," she replied. "It's been raining every day. We're in the middle of the monsoon season."

"Have you met the other actors?"

"I've made friends with Edward Woodward's girl friend, Michelle. He and I have a lot of scenes together. He's an

English actor, trained on the stage. They're all so experienced, I feel in over my head."

"You'll do great," I said. "I know you will."

"I wish you were here with me." After a pause, she added, "Would you like to come to Bangkok?"

She didn't need to ask me twice. I secured my visa from the Royal Thai Consulate, and left for Thailand. When I arrived, Bangkok International was jammed with every nationality imaginable. It was a familiar atmosphere to me, and I reveled in it, remembering all my years abroad. I made my way through the crowd, stepping over luggage and crying children and going around people who were sitting on the floor having their tea. In foreign airports total chaos reigns, but no one seems to mind.

Passing through customs, I spotted Priscilla in the crowd. She was beaming at me. Humbly standing beside her was a white-uniformed chauffeur. He took my bag, and Priscilla presented me with a bouquet of orchids and ginger blossoms.

"I've missed you so much," she said. "My teacher, my lover."

"I was going crazy being away from you," I said, sweeping her into my arms, kissing her, crushing the flowers, and lifting her off the floor. She was breathtaking, as beautiful as she'd been the day we met. She was dressed in blue Thai silk, and her eyes were electric.

We got into a waiting limo, and drove through the congested streets to the Oriental Hotel. Inside, we passed through an elegant lobby full of soaring palms and frangipani. Upstairs on the twelfth floor, as Priscilla unlocked the door, she made me close my eyes. In a moment, I heard her drawing apart the drapes.

"Okay, you can look now."

She was standing beside a large window that framed a spectacular view of Bangkok. I moved behind her, encircling her tiny waist with my arms. Below us, the city was glistening with lights.

"I have Dom Perignon chilled for you," she said, turning around.

The dark red of her upper lipstick outline accentuated the fullness of her lips. My mouth went to hers fiercely. I took her right there by the window.

Later, still standing by the window, sipping our champagne, we watched the water taxis on the river below as they went back and forth between Bangkok and its sister city, Thonburi.

"We can have supper brought to the room or meet everyone downstairs at The Captain's Table."

"I'm not tired," I said, draining my glass.

"I'd like Hall Bartlett to meet you. He's the director, and I've told him all about you."

"I'll bet you have," I said, joking. "Did you show him my pictures, like you did Julio?"

"No, I didn't," she said, laughing. "But I thought about it."

On the way down to the restaurant, Priscilla told me that disagreements had arisen between Hall and Michael Landon. Landon was not only the star but also coproducer with Hall, and they were beginning to have disagreements over the direction of the film.

"Michael's background is in TV, and he's used to very few takes," she said. "Hall works differently. He's slower. It's a frightening situation, and I don't know how to handle it."

"Stick with your director," I said. "He's the boss."

"What if there's a battle for control, and the director loses?"

"I can't answer that one."

The Captain's Table was decorated with antique nautical equipment and had crisp navy-blue tablecloths. Hall was seated at the head of what was obviously the best table in the room. It overlooked the river. He was surrounded by various members of the cast and crew, as well as his daughter and her fiancé, both of whom had parts in the film. Jergen was there, and I complimented him on his performance in *Das Boot*, but Michael Landon was not present; he was off with his own entourage.

"Priscilla has said many nice things about you," Hall said, rising from his chair. "I've been looking forward to your arrival!"

His alert gray eyes held me. There was a direct and self-assured manner about him that would have been intimidating were it not for his friendly smile. I took to him immediately.

After dinner, he told Priscilla he wouldn't be using her for the next three days.

"If you and Michael leave Bangkok, however, please notify the production office," he said. "And make sure you don't get stuck somewhere."

"I was thinking of taking Michael to Chieng Mai and then driving on up to the Burmese border."

"Be cautious," Hall said. "There have been uprisings among the opium warlords lately. They run that part of the world."

My ears perked up at the mention of warlords—and the thought of danger and adventure. After dinner, I took Priscilla aside and convinced her we had to make plane reservations to Chieng Mai for the next morning.

Starting at sunrise, we took a tour of the Chao Phraya River before flying to Chieng Mai. Inside the little open-air houses that crowded the banks, women were busily fixing breakfast over smoking hibachis as their families crawled out of bed and rolled up the bamboo shades. Each house had a rickety porch at water level, and standing on one of them was a man relieving himself into the river. Further down someone was brushing his teeth. And still further, others were washing clothes, bathing, and scrubbing pots, all from the same water. I envied them and their simple way of life on the river. They were chattering and laughing and bustling about and teasing and flirting.

"I'd love to live on this river for a while," I said.

"I bet you would," Priscilla said, laughing. "Just so you could pee in it."

"Spending some time in a place like this would be a good experience for Lisa."

"She would die if we brought her here and told her this was our new home. She's so finicky."

"It would change her life. We ought to think about it."

That afternoon we flew to Chieng Mai. We took the hotel limo and soon we were speeding to the Burmese border. Priscilla had heard that you could buy old silver jewelry from gypsies living in the mountains. We drove as far as we could, until the road became one big mass of mud. We convinced our reluctant chauffeur to walk with us far into the mountains. Removing our shoes and rolling up our trousers, we trod through ankle-deep mud until we came to a gypsy camp in a clearing. The women wore brightly colored, pleated dresses and embroidered indigo wraps. We explained that we'd come to buy silver.

They brought out typical tourist junk, but we told them that we wanted "old things." They took us back into one of their makeshift dwellings, a filthy rat's nest, and laid out a king's ransom in wares, ivory-inlaid boxes, ornate silver containers, and solid silver necklaces and bracelets. Priscilla bargained shrewdly, and we carried off a load of prizes.

We'd parked next to a rice paddy, and before climbing back in the car I took Priscilla into the water to wash off the mud. The driver refused my invitation to join us.

"I don't think we should go in there," Priscilla said. "The driver seems apprehensive."

"A rice paddy can't hurt you," I said.

Priscilla tiptoed to the edge, dabbing at the mud, and quickly backed out. I went in up to my knees, vigorously splashing around.

"There! You see? Nothing to it!"

As I emerged from the rice paddy, Priscilla gasped, "Oh, my God! Look at your legs!"

My calves were covered with leeches. The driver tried burning them off with his cigarette lighter, but all he succeeded in burning was me.

"No telling what diseases they carry," Priscilla said.

"Leeches are harmless. In ancient times, doctors used them to cure everything."

I yanked them off, and blood began trickling down my legs.

It was getting late, and there was just enough time to reach the border before nightfall. The driver was hesitant, warning us of the possibility of bandit raids after dark, but we pressed on, fishtailing down the slippery road. Between breaks in the bamboo hedge that lined the river, we could see shacks scattered along the bank.

"That's where the opium people live," the driver said. "We are not safe here."

At that moment, the tires began spinning and we found ourselves stuck in a foot of mud.

"Please remove your jewelry and be very quiet," the driver ordered.

"What's the problem?" I asked.

"Do as he says," Priscilla said.

She was looking in the direction of the bamboo hedge. Men with bloodshot eyes and swollen faces were coming through it and heading in our direction. Nearly naked, they had tattoos and scars from self-mutilation on their chests, shoulders, and arms.

"They look like zombies," she said.

The driver hid his valuables and got out of the car.

"We're in trouble," Priscilla said.

"Crawl down on the floor."

"What if I don't make it back for my movie?"

I covered her with my jacket, and from underneath it came her muffled voice: "I don't believe this is happening to me."

"Be quiet! Don't move! Someone's coming over here."

One of the opium people walked up to the car and pressed his face against the window, staring at me angrily. I wasn't sure if I was right in staring back at him, but instinct told me to stare him down. He tried the door handle, but it was locked. He scooped up a handful of mud, smeared the window with it, and then went away. I felt the car bouncing up and down and looked back. Several men were on the bumper and others were shaking the sides of the car. They were arguing with our driver, pushing him around, but stopped abruptly when he reached in his pocket and produced some money. He got back in the car, started the engine, and the opium people pushed us out of the mud. Then they started throwing mud and rocks after us.

"A lot of bad things happen in this region," he said as we sped off. "Nobody stops in their territory."

"Can we go on up to the border?" I asked.

"Are you crazy?" Priscilla shrieked, climbing back up on the seat.

"I'm only joking."

We found the main road and began the three-hour drive back to Chieng Mai.

The following morning, we returned to Bangkok and discovered that the film was in big trouble. Hall Bartlett and Michael Landon weren't speaking, and people were saying that the film was close to shutting down. In addition to the tension in the company, the rains had come again, and tempers were flaring.

That evening, in the red-light district of Patpong, in a smoke-filled bar, we watched smooth-skinned strippers bumping and grinding. Some people at the next table were talking about "the dirtiest show in Asia," and when I asked them where it was, they invited us to come with them.

"We can walk there," one of them said. "It's not far from here. But it might be too raunchy for your lady."

"I'll be the judge of that," Priscilla said, smiling.

A short distance away we found the club, and a fat man at the door demanded twenty-five dollars per person. Inside, the show was already underway. A girl with long, black shiny braids was squatting on the floor, opening a soft-drink bottle with her vagina. She sucked the drink into her, then walked around without it dripping. As she started refilling the bottle from her vagina, I asked Priscilla if she wanted to leave.

"Not yet. There was a club like this in Germany, and

Elvis took me there. Let's stay a few more minutes. I can't believe she's able to do that."

Priscilla was captivated by the woman's capabilities. I was, too, but I'd seen this sort of thing before. When another girl climbed on the stage and began picking up coins between her legs, I told Priscilla we were going.

We had to get up early to practice her dive at the British Club. The pool we were using had a lousy diving board, and to make matters worse, word had gotten out that Priscilla Presley was going to be diving, and a crowd had formed. Her jitters came back, and she didn't want to practice in front of everybody. I gave her my Walkman, turned up Gladys Knight's "Jump to It," got a draft beer and insisted she drink it. Five minutes later, she was springing off the board.

Everyone was prepared for a long day, expecting numerous takes, but Priscilla performed well immediately. Hall was impressed, and Priscilla told him I'd acted like a drill sergeant while teaching her to dive at UCLA.

"It was worth it," Hall said. "You did great."

She was looking forward to working with Edward Woodward. When they did their scene, however, I could see that Priscilla was in trouble. During a break, she asked me if I could run lines with her.

"He's so controlled," she said. "I can't get a connection. I feel stiff with him."

"On the next take," I told her, "take his hand and hold it and make him look at you. Then seduce him with your eyes."

"What if he pulls away?"

"Don't let go."

"Are you sure?"

"He's British. It'll get to him."

When they resumed, Priscilla took his hand, which got his full attention. After the take, she looked over at me and nodded.

The last location in Thailand was down in the south. We were ferried from the village of Pouquet to a little island. Hall started shooting a love scene between Priscilla and Landon, in which they were both in bathing suits. Suddenly, Landon refused to work. He wouldn't take Hall's direction. The two of them glared at each other in the burning sun as the movie ground to a standstill.

This was the moment of truth for Hall—he had a possible mutiny on his hands. As they stood there, locked in conflict, I watched them for a moment, wondering what, if anything, I should do. Hall held his position, perspiration streaming down his face. Michael looked comfortable and nonchalant in his swimming suit, casually enjoying a beer.

I walked over to an ice chest and opened up a bottle of soda water. I brought it back to Hall and handed it to him. He looked surprised but took it gratefully. Then I stood by his side.

I looked over at Priscilla, but she took refuge with the makeup lady. She wasn't getting involved. We were very different people when it came to loyalty, I realized.

Hall took his time drinking the soda, considering his next move. He remained cool under pressure, letting Landon have his way. After a few minutes Hall turned to his assistant director and told him to get the actors back on the set. Priscilla returned immediately, but Landon ignored Hall and finished his beer.

Hall got behind the camera and started directing the scene without Landon. When Landon saw what was going on, he came back to the set, and Hall Bartlett shouted, "Roll 'em!"

* * *

At the window in our suite at the Oriental, I looked down on the Chao Phraya for the last time. There was a full moon over the river, and it seemed to be beckoning me to stay. Priscilla would be shooting the remainder of her film in Florida and the Bahamas, and I was going back home alone. She'd asked me to accompany her, and I both wanted to and didn't want to. While it would have been great skin-diving in the West Indies as she wrapped the film, something kept holding me back. I was indecisive, and couldn't make up my mind about our continuing together. Year four was upon us, and even though we didn't know how it had happened, somehow Priscilla and Lisa and I had definitely become a family and I couldn't let go of that.

32

Back in L.A., I took Lisa and her boyfriend to the movies. On the way home, they asked if they could sit in the back seat of the car. I adjusted the rearview mirror and saw that my little girl had grown up. I was happy for her and also liked her choice of a boyfriend. He was a wholesome, polite kid, someone I would have been happy to see Caroline with. Glancing up into the mirror, Lisa caught me looking at them as they made out.

"I see you, Merkley," she said.

Lisa was beginning to display many of her mother's traits. They were both very private people, but very romantic too. I wondered if guys would be attracted to Lisa mainly because she was Elvis's daughter. Was that boy in the back seat now feeling the same joy I'd felt when I'd won Priscilla? And what would he do when he discovered the human being squirming ambivalently behind the Presley name?

Thinking about Priscilla and me, I realized that from our youth both of us had had many things come our way because of our looks, and we'd unwittingly let that asset become our guide. So much is automatically offered to good-looking people that it can distort your perspective, making you take shortcuts rather than develop yourself. When things come to you too easily, you miss the whole process of life. It can be exciting but it also leaves you unfulfilled, immature and unable to cope with reality. This had kept me from becoming who I truly wanted to be—a normal, loving father and husband. With Priscilla, I could have had real love, but the thrill of stepping into Elvis's shoes had taken over and wreaked havoc.

Elvis had created her for me, I sometimes thought, often telling Priscilla, "He molded you into this perfect woman and then let you slip between his fingers."

Priscilla confided to me that her greatest fear was falling victim to a fortune hunter. We were both lucky that I had no desire to marry a woman for her money.

Our perpetual, unremitting love life had been the devil's making. We'd become like two animals snared in a trap—snarling, eyes bulging and berserk, twitching and jerking. Our world was completely off kilter.

The big house, fine cars, tennis court, pool, people attending us around the clock—none of this could get you the moon over the Chao Phraya. Or even a little bit of serenity. That, I now realized, was what I wanted.

Again I looked back at Lisa in the car with her boyfriend and remembered my first steady girl in high school. When Betty Lynn and I had broken up, something snapped inside and I'd started drinking more heavily, convinced that love would only betray me and bring me pain. Now I wanted to start my life over and become the trusting person I was back in high school, before I felt love had failed me.

When Priscilla's movie was finished, she returned from

the final location in the Bahamas, tan and glowing and confident—and distant. I knew there was someone else.

We argued, but now there was a difference—we didn't make up later. I got very busy with my acting career, vowing not to let our relationship get in the way this time. I landed another film role, in *Paper Dolls*, starring Daryl Hannah, and I was scoring major TV commercials left and right—Taylor Wine, Honda, Chevrolet. Priscilla, meanwhile, wasn't working, and she was shopping compulsively every day. I thought she was just restless because of post-film depression and would get over it. But when she started mysteriously disappearing for whole days, and then returning flushed and flustered in the evenings, I began playing detective. Though I hadn't moved back in, I frequently spent the night. One morning, before she left the house dressed to kill, I checked the mileage on her car. That evening, the odometer showed she'd gone more than 150 miles. I asked her what she'd done that day and she became defensive, replying, "Nothing important."

"Who are you seeing?"

Her face went blank. I had caught her. She told me she'd driven down south to have lunch with a stuntman from her film, but it was "nothing serious." And, she added, it was finished. I dropped it.

For my birthday in September, she took me to Touch, a private supper club. Again there was an intimacy between us and I felt that our love was rekindled. After dinner, we went on to another club, La Cage aux Folles, where Priscilla had put together a surprise party for me. I looked around at the guests—agents, managers, and our interior decorator—and noticed there wasn't a single person there who didn't work for us. They all sang "Happy Birthday" to me, and I wondered if I'd get a bill for it the next day.

During the floor show, someone in the party asked Priscilla how her parents had liked La Cage when she'd brought them there several months ago. In answering, she let it slip out that the actor she'd had an affair with in class had been with them that evening. I pretended not to hear this, but fury swept over me like molten lava.

Despite the precariousness of our relationship, my working steadily brought some kind of stability back, and Priscilla was happy with me again. We decided to give it another chance, and I moved back into her house. I'd missed the elegance, star treatment, and refuge behind the big black barricade, having grown accustomed to this high standard of living. I'd constructed a persona, just as Elvis had, and so far it seemed to be working for me in my quest to become a star. The only problem was that I wanted to grow, but I felt I was stagnating.

Trying to pull us together and bring back some of the lightness and fun that we'd had when we'd first got together, I did something rather absurd one night. A group of us was having dinner at a Greek restaurant in East L.A. It was a seedy part of town but the restaurants were known for great ethnic cuisine. The food at this particular restaurant turned out to be horrible, and the belly dancer, shaking her stomach to a scratchy record, was even worse. I wasn't about to let this boredom continue, and since no one else at the table seemed to be doing anything about it, when the dancer finished I excused myself from our table and went up to the men's room.

I undressed in the stall down to my birthday suit, then wrapped myself from head to toe in toilet paper. I came back downstairs, selected a record, and began to do my version of the Greek dance. Everyone in the place went along with my act, thinking I was part of the show. They clapped along until the toilet paper started unwinding. From our table I heard Lisa say, "Oh, God, Mommy! It's Michael!"

I continued dancing, letting the toilet paper unwind until all that was left was a little around my groin. Glancing over at our table, I saw an array of reactions, ranging between horror, disbelief, and laughter. Holding a handful of toilet paper over my crotch, keeping myself covered, I bowed to the audience, took the record off, returned it to its stack, then went up to the john and got dressed. I returned to the table and sat down. The other diners seemed to make no connection between me and the naked madman who'd entertained them only minutes earlier. Priscilla was laughing about it, as was everyone else at the table now.

"We never have to worry about a boring time when Michael's there," Priscilla said, but I detected a trace of sarcasm in her voice.

I suddenly realized I was having to do wild and crazy things again to be happy. I didn't like it. In a dream I had one night, I was with Elvis in Palm Springs, and we were sitting on his bed, both of us wearing matching white terry-cloth bathrobes.

"I'll tell you a secret if you won't repeat it to anyone," Elvis said.

I swore I wouldn't.

"I've been finding lots of hair in my brush," he said.

"No big deal," I said. "Mine fell out once, but I massaged my scalp with Vaseline and it grew back."

Admiring my full head of hair, he said, "Show me how to do it."

"You must massage your scalp for exactly seven minutes after showering."

Elvis went into the bathroom, got in the shower, and hollered for me to join him. I did, and as I was lathering his hair, Priscilla peeked in at us. She was wrapped in a Roman toga and holding a bunch of grapes, and had long bangs, cut just above her eyes, which were glaring angrily.

"Come on in here, Cilla," he said.

"You should be ashamed of yourself," she said, throwing the grapes at us. "I don't have time for frivolity. I'm already late for my meeting at MGM with the Colonel."

She stormed off.

Elvis went into a fit, yanking on his hair so hard that it all fell out.

"Take your own guitar," he screamed after her. Turning to me, he said, "Her problem is she thinks she can sing, but she can't even carry a tune."

I'd seen the dream as a sign. Though we were back living together, our relationship was clearly out of control, and Priscilla and I were going our own ways.

Even nightmares fade with time, and soon Christmas was upon us. Though we both knew we were on a sinking ship, we stubbornly held on, continuing to observe family traditions together. For Christmas, I planned a ski trip to Mount Crested Butte in Colorado, where Priscilla and I had once owned condos. Before leaving, we spent Christmas Eve at the Polo Lounge in L.A., having champagne and caviar, and the next day we had Christmas dinner with Priscilla's parents in Brentwood. On our way home, we started arguing. I'd drunk too much at dinner, and Priscilla was upset.

"Your drinking's wearing me down," she said. "You've got to do something about it."

"Stop trying to control me. I can quit any time I want."

"You're a different person when you drink, Michael, someone I don't want to know."

"You don't know anyone anyway," I said. "We have absolutely no friends—except for publicists, agents, managers, and photographers. And they're only around because we pay them."

"We need them for our careers," she pointed out.

"We used to be around all kinds of people. It didn't matter what they did."

"See anyone you like. I'm not stopping you."

"I want *us* to do it, Priscilla. I need people, all kinds of people."

"I can't live like that anymore."

"You mean, you're a star now?"

"Things have changed. One day, you'll understand."

"All I understand is that you're starting to act like a prima donna."

Our ski trip to Colorado went completely haywire. On the third night, after dinner and a couple of bottles of red wine, which always made me crazy, we returned to the condo. I brought the mattress into the living room and put it in front of the fireplace, a ritual we'd been fond of ever since the Fire Island weekend.

We lay there listening to the crackling fire and watching the snow fall outside the window. Soon, we started making love. Everything was going fine until Priscilla did something that reminded me of the actor she'd had an affair with. She'd once told me that she didn't like his breath, that it always smelled of tobacco. Now, as we were making love, she said, "I hope my breath doesn't smell of garlic."

I rolled off her, tortured by the image of her kissing the

actor that day in class, and said, "How could you make love to him right under my nose?"

"Who? What are you talking about?"

"That actor."

"*What* actor?"

"That idiot in class."

"You're not bringing him up again!"

"And I can't believe you introduced him to your parents. You took him to La Cage aux Folles, flaunting him in front of everybody!"

Priscilla could see that I was getting very upset. She moved away to the far edge of the mattress.

"You let him shove his ugly, nasty tongue down your throat! The whole class turned to see my reaction! And you'd just slept with him the day before."

"Michael, stop."

"How many times did you do it?"

"You're breaking our agreement. We got all this out at Scientology."

"You even had me help you with the scene! I worked with you for days, showing you what to do, how to say your lines, and then you went off and fucked him."

I jerked the mattress up, she tumbled off it, and I threw it at her. Then I grabbed her and wrestled her to the floor, squeezing her hard.

"Damn you, Priscilla! Damn you!"

"Michael, don't! You'll kill me! I can't breathe! You're choking me!"

"Damn you, Priscilla! I loved you so much."

I threw her back down onto the mattress.

"Oh, God, Michael! You've hurt my neck! I can't move!"

I rushed over to her.

"Don't touch me!" she screamed.

I ran into the bathroom to get her a wet towel. When I came back, she was gone. I searched the condo and out in the hallway, but she was nowhere in sight. I called her name frantically, but there was no reply.

I ran outside in the snow barefooted and wearing only pajama bottoms. I knew Priscilla was in a skimpy nightie and couldn't have gone far. I tramped around in the snow, calling out her name. I was panicking. Finally, I found her hiding underneath the condo. She was cowering and trembling behind a big pile of firewood.

"Please don't hurt me," she cried.

"Oh, God, Priscilla! Forgive me. I love you so much I just go crazy with jealousy. Come to me, baby."

"If you promise not to hurt me again."

She came out slowly, and I took her in my arms. She was frozen.

We went back into the condo and sat by the fire. We were silent except for the chattering of our teeth.

"What are we going to do?" I asked.

"I don't know," she said, barely audible.

"We'll kill each other one day if this keeps up. We've got to figure out a way to separate for good."

She sat there holding her neck in pain.

"I can't even cry," I said. "I feel empty. Let's go back to L.A. tomorrow."

"If you want to."

"I do. It's my fault. I just can't let it go—you and that guy . . . and so many other things."

"Michael, don't start again!"

"No, baby. I won't. I'm just so unhappy that we can't make it work out anymore."

When we calmed down, she said, "I want to die. I can't take it anymore."

We fell into each other's arms, sobbing.

The emotional intensity of that weekend left us drained and empty, yet, somehow, still clinging to each other. We returned to L.A. and our lives went on.

33

Lisa was now well settled into her second year of private school in Ojai, California. Priscilla and I had different attitudes toward raising kids and often fought over the subject. Mine was one of leniency and permissiveness. I felt that children should be allowed to make their own choices so long as they were willing to listen to my viewpoint first. I told Priscilla it was better to let Lisa experience things and not constantly hide her away, protecting her from life. Later, when she grew up and had to face the world on her own, she'd be able to make her own decisions and not always have to run back to Mommy. But Priscilla preferred keeping Lisa under her wing.

We got tired of going to Palm Springs for the weekends, and since Lisa was at school in Ojai, Priscilla decided to buy a house in nearby Montecito. She wanted to remain as close to Lisa as possible. On weekends Lisa could spend time with us, and Montecito provided a solution.

Lisa revealed something that shocked me.

"There are more drugs available in this private school

than in any school I've ever attended in L.A.," she said.

"Are you into drugs, Lisa?" I asked.

"No, but everything is available there."

Lisa's new flame was an older boy, in his twenties, and they'd recently started dating. He was so charming and polite he had Priscilla wrapped around his little finger. He was extremely affectionate, and Priscilla returned his hugs with equal warmth and exuberance.

I was envious, seeing the three of them becoming so chummy. But I still liked him. His cocky personality reminded me so much of my own when I'd first met Priscilla five years earlier. I thought he wanted the mother as well as the daughter. He was constantly hugging and cuddling them both and baby-talking with them. Priscilla enjoyed his attention thoroughly, and when I told her I thought she was being too friendly, she dismissed the notion.

"Don't be so serious, Michael," she said. "He's Lisa's *boyfriend.*"

I asked Lisa if she felt bothered by how friendly he and her mother were becoming. "Does it upset you?" I asked. She wouldn't answer me, turning her head away.

Soon the bubble burst when Lisa found out how unfaithful and deceitful her boyfriend was. Priscilla was very upset.

I told Priscilla I understood her anger and disappointment but added that I thought it would be unfair if she totally blamed Lisa's boyfriend. Lisa had not been coerced into anything. She had gone along with him, and in fact still wanted to be with him, just as Priscilla herself had rebelled against her parents when they'd tried to prevent her from seeing Elvis. I reminded Priscilla that none of this would have happened if she hadn't been so protective about Lisa's every move, that it was natural that Lisa would want to experience everything all at once with the first opportunity that presented itself. And he'd been it.

Priscilla stared at me in disbelief.

"Keep out of this!" she said. "Don't try to control me and my daughter! You're always trying to make me do things your way! I'm sick and tired of it! Elvis did the same thing. No man will ever control me again! You think it's okay for men to run around, but let me do it, and you condemn me for life. Just stay out of our life."

Her tears were flowing.

"I'm not taking it anymore," she screamed.

I took her into my arms. She was crying uncontrollably by now.

"What's happened to my little girl, Michael? She's grown away from me. I've lost her."

"Priscilla, you have to let her go. Let her grow up."

Her body went stiff.

"You're doing it again," she said. "You're trying to control me!"

A couple of evenings later, we were at a party at John Schlesinger's house up Sunset Plaza Drive. I'd admired John's work ever since *Yanks*, which Richard Gere had starred in, and Richard was at the party that night. I was curious about him because people so often said we looked alike. I found him rather introverted, but we had a pleasant conversation. I left Priscilla and Gere talking by themselves and Priscilla later remarked to me that we were more than similar—we could be brothers, she said. The main difference was that I liked to go unshaven for days at a time, and Gere was clean-shaven.

"He's also a Virgo," she said, "and he talks with his

hands like you. You two are so much alike I couldn't believe it. Even his skin is smooth like yours."

I knew that when a woman looked that close at a man's face, she was up to more than making idle comparisons.

Some time after John's party, I was leaving for a shoot in Palm Springs for *Gentlemen's Quarterly* and asked Priscilla to stop by my condo that evening to say good-bye. I'd been spending a lot of time in my condo.

"I've had a lot of time to think about us," I told her.

"So have I, Michael, and—"

"God, I miss you so much! Come to Palm Springs with me. Tonight."

"I'd love to Michael, but the new lawyer for the estate is here from New York, and we're meeting at Trumps. Then I'm meeting my agent for dinner at Morton's."

"Just you and he?"

"Michael! He's my agent! He's been working on something for me."

"I'm happy for you, baby. I'm sorry I snapped at you."

"I'm beginning to feel good about us again. Call me from the Springs—I'm sure I won't be out too late. I'll miss you."

That night in Palm Springs, after dining with the crew, I slipped off to the pool with a model from the Ford Agency. I had no intentions other than taking a swim with her and then enjoying the Jacuzzi, but once we were in the hot steaming water, she started massaging my shoulders and I felt that old familiar stirring. We wound up kissing, and I asked her to come to my room.

"I'm married," she said, "but I love the way you kiss. Let's just stay in the Jacuzzi."

We stayed in there for hours, and I tried every way I

could think of to seduce her, but she would only let me kiss her and touch her breasts. I returned to my room weak-kneed and masturbated.

I called Priscilla around midnight, but there was no answer in Beverly Hills. I tried to go to sleep but tossed and turned, feeling guilty, and began to wonder why she was out so late. At 1:30 A.M. I called again. Still there was no answer. Finally, at daybreak, she picked up the phone.

"I had the phone turned down and couldn't hear it," she explained, a little out of breath. I wanted to believe her, but I was too familiar with the phones in the house.

"You can't turn it down that low," I said.

"I can't talk right now. I have to get Lisa up."

"Priscilla, since when does Lisa get up at six-thirty in the morning?"

There was a silence, and then I could hear her muffled sobs. I asked her what had happened, but I already knew.

"Michael, I drank too much. Richard Gere stopped by our table after dinner. We're represented by the same agent. After a while, everyone left and it was just me and Richard. We had cognacs, and you know how much I hate cognac."

I sure did. She'd never drink it with me, always saying, "You'd might as well be drinking gasoline."

"When we finally left and went outside to get our cars," Priscilla said, "he asked me where I was going. I told him, 'Home.' He shook his head, grinned at me and said, 'No, you're not.' I found myself in his car, heading for Bob Evans's house, where he was staying as a houseguest. I can't remember anything very clearly after that, except for feeling drunk and dizzy. The next morning, I woke up, naked in bed beside him, my clothes and his scattered all over the floor. I had a pounding headache, and my first thought was that I'd left Lisa alone all night. I'd never done that in my life."

Her car was still at Morton's, she said. She borrowed Richard's car, which turned out to be Bob Evans's, and drove home to check on Lisa, shower, clean up, and pull herself together. As she entered the house, the phone was ringing. It was me.

Later, when I returned from Palm Springs and we discussed it face to face in her bedroom, she claimed all she could remember of the evening was Richard kissing her as he undressed her in the doorway to his bedroom, carrying her to bed, and feeling him on top of her.

I didn't care any more. I felt empty.

The next day she sounded heartbroken, saying Gere hadn't phoned. She sent him a letter through her private secretary telling him how disappointed she was that he hadn't even had the courtesy to call and ask how she felt; she wasn't a common whore, and how dare he treat her that way?

The princess I'd put on a pedestal finally came tumbling down. I felt sorry for her, yet realized there was nothing I could do to ease her pain over having been treated badly. Guys do that. I'd done it so many times in the past that it made me think of all the women I must have hurt for one evening of lust. But I couldn't help smiling, each time I thought of Richard and Priscilla. It happens to the best of us.

A few days later, Lisa and I had a heart-to-heart about her boyfriend. She said he'd had her mind really screwed up. And now he'd told her to leave him alone, he didn't want to see her any more. He'd met someone else and she should do the same. I watched the tears running down her face and shared the pain she was feeling. I told her it was better that it had happened this way, instead of after marriage and possibly a baby. She said she didn't care about anything, she just wanted to get over him, but she couldn't seem to do it.

"I'll never love like that again, Merkley," she said.

"I know how you feel," I said. "But don't give up on love, Lisa. You're only sixteen and have many wonderful things ahead of you, especially true love. Someday, you'll meet someone who deserves you. Just be strong, and hold on."

"Do you think he really hates me?"

"Nobody could hate you."

"I think he does."

I found it hard to console Lisa with words. She was so young and so vulnerable, yet at the same time, I knew she was very much like Elvis. She would survive. But for how long, and with what kind of existence? I worried about that.

"Your father was very special," I said. "And I know how difficult it can be to try to live with people only looking at you as his daughter. But you're much more than that. In the years we've lived together, your mother, you, and me, I've watched you grow and I love you as much as my own daughter."

She touched my hand. "Thank you, Merky," she said.

"As time goes on, it gets easier. I promise you. Life is an adventure. It's all up to you whether it's fun or filled with pain."

"Don't get too serious, Mickney. I feel better now."

She gave me a hug and told me she loved me. I hugged her back. And never in my life had I ever felt a stronger love for anyone than I did for Lisa at that moment.

34

Priscilla and I began doing crazy things—anything to forget our bad times and fill the void we now faced. Flying to Shelbyville, Tennessee, for a horse show, the "Celebration," we bought a champion colt, Ebony's Secret Threat, for $15,000. We were guests of honor, and Priscilla was presenting Elvis's champion Tennessee Walker in a special event. Stabled at Graceland since Elvis's death, the horse had been brought out of retirement and retrained for one last show.

Though I looked like a millionaire in high society, I wasn't. And with the inside-out state that Priscilla and I had reached, I'd become fed up with everything. Modeling, TV commercials, and acting. I couldn't find the will to go after them any more. As a result, the offers were now few. I started looking for a regular job and even applied for work as a window dresser at Saks Fifth Avenue on Wilshire Boulevard. They said I didn't have enough experience. That made me laugh.

When Priscilla invited me to accompany her to Australia

on a publicity trip, I borrowed a large sum of money to cover my expenses. As long as you keep your face out there, I figured, and are willing to take a risk, you're still in the running. I wasn't defeated yet. Also, I was willing to go to any length to avoid facing the mess we were in.

On our return from the Outback, I looked rugged, beat, sunbaked, and bedraggled—coincidentally the very look Kent Cigarettes wanted and had been searching for the world over. For their image, they needed rugged elegance, and I fit the bill. They signed me to an exclusive, six-figure contract for five years as the Kent Man. I was back on my feet again.

The business never ceased to amaze me. When I saw Nina, she said, "Contracts don't come around that often. Especially for men. You're very lucky. And—it's a biggie." It also meant a big commission for her, which made me feel good. I'd been at the top so long that I had come to enjoy the feeling of walking into the agency, knowing that I was again one of their biggest moneymakers.

Something funny happens when you achieve a goal. It's suddenly no longer a big deal, and you're left at a loss for what to do the next day for excitement. Kent soon took care of that, sending me off to the Caribbean for two weeks to shoot the first round of commercials. Even though Priscilla and I hadn't been able to settle our differences, travel was one thing we would always put our troubles aside for. I flew Priscilla to St. John's Island, happy to be able to show off my new status as the Kent Man. I was given V.I.P. treatment everywhere, and I loved it. Priscilla and I would go back to our elegant suite in the evening after dinner and laugh like crazy about my new role. It was an attitude I could play well—the suave cigarette smoker, the continental type, the man about town all the girls wanted and all the men wanted to be like. I was content.

And, soon, so was Priscilla. She landed a contract as a regular on *Dallas*, the most popular TV show in the world. Like addicts who'd got their fix, we were contented once more and I moved back into the house. With both of us working steadily we were going smooth, like a seaplane gliding on a glassy lake.

I joined Priscilla in Dallas, Texas, during her first season on the show. Larry Hagman, Priscilla, and I all stayed at the luxurious Mansion on Turtle Creek hotel. Evenings, I helped her run her lines for the role of Jenna Wade. She was scared but excited and determined to prove herself as a dramatic actress.

During the daytime, when Priscilla was filming, I hung out at the pool, memorizing my lines for a play I was scheduled to appear in. Larry Hagman was down at the pool one day and I introduced myself, telling him I liked his hat. It was a crazy hat with a battery-run fan to keep him cool in the sweltering Texas heat. Larry asked me if I was in the show, noticing that I was studying a script.

"No," I said. "It's for a play I'm doing in L.A."

"*Dallas* could use a new face, someone young and good-looking," he said. "I'll speak to the producers."

Later, I asked Priscilla to remind Larry of what he'd said, adding, "It would be great if we were on the same show together."

"I haven't been on the show long enough," Priscilla said, "but if an opportunity comes up, I'll say something."

Some time later, on a bright Sunday afternoon in

Malibu, we had brunch at the Hagman's, but nothing further was ever said about putting me in *Dallas*.

My play, *The Ballad of Lizard Gulch*, began rehearsals in L.A. As the lead, Bo, a knife-wielding Vietnam vet, I was a sort of modern-day Merlin the Magician. During rehearsals I used a prop knife but as opening night approached, I decided I needed a more realistic looking weapon.

A few days before the show opened, Lisa returned from summer camp in Spain. She had a gift for me, and when I opened the package, I saw a large, mean-looking, bone-handled knife with six gears. It sounded worse than a rattlesnake when you opened it.

"How did you know I needed a knife?" I asked her.

She smiled at me.

"When I saw it, something told me Merky needs a knife."

I was proud doing this show, especially one night when all the women in my life—Mother, Priscilla, Caroline, Lisa, and Nina—were in the audience, watching me. The critics gave us good reviews, and the show had a successful run.

During this period, Priscilla told me she was thinking about writing a book about her life with Elvis. She said the Presley name had been more of a hindrance than a help in her career, and maybe the book would set her free once and for all. I encouraged her, telling her to do it. A few days later she decided, "I don't want to. Everyone's writing books about him."

"But you're the only person who knows the true story. You're always talking about wanting to be free from Elvis. This is the chance to do it."

"You don't understand, Michael. I've lived a life that no one will ever live again. There are things I'd be afraid to reveal, things that his fans might be upset about."

"What are you concerned about? The fans, or yourself? And what about Lisa? Doesn't she deserve to be free, too?"

"People will say I'm cashing in."

"So fucking what? Do you have anything to be afraid of?"

"No."

"Then write it. I'll help you."

"I don't know if I can do it."

"You remember how scared you were when you were on the diving board? If you were able to break through that fear, doing a book will be simple."

"Would you really help me write it?"

"All the way. I swear to God."

There was no further mention of the book. Then one day she came to me and told me she'd decided to do it. I warned her to be prepared for a gut-wrenching experience. It turned out to be traumatic for me as well. Many times during the writing of the book, I felt like I was watching a scene straight out of *The Exorcist*. As she relived her past, she became both Elvis and the person she'd been when they'd lived together.

After months of grueling work, Priscilla needed a break —and so did I. I suppose we thought once again travel could cure our depression. We went to Africa on safari, exploring the wilderness, watching lions, leopards, and incredible sunsets over the plains, and making desperate love. We videotaped it all, somehow knowing that the last granules of hope were about to sift through the hourglass.

35

Priscilla was unbeatable when it came to keeping up family traditions such as birthdays, Easter egg hunts, and especially Christmas gatherings. She told me that she'd loved it when she and Elvis and Lisa and the whole family, including the guys and their girls and wives, got together on the holidays and celebrated at home. Her parents were the same way, and when she told them that she wouldn't be spending Christmas with them, that she and Lisa were going to be in Florida with me and my family, they were disappointed.

On our way to Pensacola, we discussed the state of our relationship, and I said to Priscilla, "We're like puppets on the end of a string, letting the wind blow us around."

She seemed surprised and said, "I thought we were doing fine now."

"I'm not saying we're not doing good. We just don't have a definite direction."

"Our careers are going well, Michael, why not just be happy with that for a while?"

* * *

One night in Florida during the holidays, I took us all out to dinner. I convinced Priscilla to let our daughters, Lisa and Caroline, each have a glass of champagne. We were all in good spirits, and after the meal Priscilla agreed to let Lisa go with Caroline to meet her boyfriend and go dancing. The girls would then spend the night with Grace, my ex-wife, where Caroline lived. The only stipulation Priscilla made was that Lisa and Caroline be in by midnight—and no drinking.

I told Caroline she had to give me her word that she'd respect Priscilla's demand. I explained that it was very important that we have a wonderful Christmas holiday together, and I'd appreciate it if she and Lisa didn't cause any hassles. Caroline promised.

Priscilla and I were staying at my mother's home, and the girls called there around midnight.

"We're home!" Lisa said to Priscilla, lying.

What had actually happened was that the girls had gone to a bar. Caroline had no problem getting in because the bouncer at the door was a friend of hers, and she was able to convince him to also let Lisa in. Once inside, they started drinking, dancing, and having a good time. Then Caroline got into a big fight with her boyfriend and he slapped her. Lisa told him he'd better watch it, he'd better leave Caroline alone or he'd be in big trouble.

"I have the power and the money to ruin you," Lisa said.

That's when the girls had called my mother's house from a pay phone and talked with Priscilla, claiming they were at Grace's. They then called Grace and Lisa convinced her that if Priscilla telephoned and asked about them, to tell her that they were already asleep. They went back into the bar and finally went home around 1:30 A.M. When they got in, the phone was ringing. I was calling. Priscilla had told me she'd heard noise in the background when Lisa had called, so we'd figured they weren't at home. Priscilla got on the phone and told Lisa, "You stay there. I'm coming to get you," and hung up. On the way over, I told Priscilla that the girls definitely needed to be disciplined. This time, they'd gone too far.

When we drove up, Lisa and Caroline were so scared they went crying into Caroline's bedroom. Grace told them not to worry, we wouldn't hurt them. I went inside the house and got the girls.

"Priscilla wants to see you both," I said.

When Priscilla saw them come to the doorway, she walked up to them.

"I'm so disgusted with you, I can't believe you," she said.

Before either one of them knew what had happened, Priscilla reared back, swung, and slapped Caroline in the face in the exact spot her boyfriend had slugged her in. Then she swung again, fast, and slapped Lisa.

Caroline turned and ran like lightning, and Lisa was directly behind her. I blocked Lisa, and Priscilla grabbed her by the hair. She dragged Lisa to the back seat of my mother's Cadillac in the driveway, where she started spanking her. Lisa was screaming at the top of her lungs, and Priscilla was trying to hold her mouth with one hand while hitting her with the other.

Grace and I were in the doorway, and Grace said, "If you don't go out there and stop that, I'm going to. I have neighbors, you know."

At that point, the police pulled up. Grace and I went out

to the patrol car and tried to explain that everything was okay, we'd just had a family misunderstanding. The cops walked up to the back of my mother's car and trained their flashlights on Priscilla and Lisa in the back seat.

Priscilla had seen the patrol car coming and when the cops asked Lisa how she was, she made Lisa say she was fine. The cops had no idea who they were investigating in the back of my mom's Cadillac.

Priscilla and Lisa left Pensacola early the next morning and flew back to L.A. I stayed behind. I wanted to talk with my daughter and straighten things out. Although I wasn't as upset as Priscilla was about the girls' lying and drinking, I knew Caroline needed my reassurance that Priscilla would get over it and forgive her.

Caroline told me she really understood and knew it was her fault.

"Lisa and I hardly ever get to see each other, so when we do, we try to pour everything into one night. I wish I got to come out there and be with you guys more often. Lisa wants me to come out there and live with her. We feel like sisters."

Caroline explained to me that Lisa had got along fine with Grace, who reminded her of the "down home" folks at Graceland, and the two of them enjoyed sitting in the living room, smoking cigarettes and chatting. Grace had lent the girls five dollars each to go out that night.

I promised Caroline that I would work on getting her out to L.A. more often. "I feel better when we're together, baby," I said. "Lately I feel like I've lost my personality. When I'm with you, I feel like me again."

"You haven't lost anything, Dad," she said, giving me a

big hug. "You've just put some things on the shelf. When you're ready, you'll take them back down."

Caroline's insight impressed me. I embraced her again and boarded my plane, and as I turned to wave good-bye, she was wiping her eyes.

36

The final breakup happened as soon as I returned to L.A. On the flight back, I had decided to make one last effort to pull Priscilla and me together into a workable relationship that involved more time together with our kids and less with our careers and personal desires. That didn't happen. Priscilla and I fought immediately and she stormed off to New York for *Night of a Hundred Stars*.

On the day she was supposed to return I went over to her house, hoping to make up. I wanted one last chance for us to put all our problems of the past behind us and start anew. As I waited for the limousine to pull up outside the gate, bringing her home, I thought of all kinds of wonderful things we'd soon be doing together—me and the kids and her. I waited and I thought and thought and thought. This time, she didn't return to me.

Hours passed, and I gave up and went home. Then two days went by, and she still hadn't returned. I took a wild guess and called Twenty-nine Palms, near Palm Springs, a luxurious spa we'd often talked about going to but never had, for some reason. I asked the desk clerk to speak to Priscilla, telling him that I was her manager and it was an emergency. His reply sent a chill up my back.

"They're still not answering," he said. "You can leave a message, but I believe they've already checked out, sir."

I knew she and whoever she was there with must be on their way back to Beverly Hills. I went back over to her house and waited. I was scared. She'd never done anything this blatant before. I hadn't eaten, literally, for days, and was chain-smoking. I tried to tell myself that she'd gone there with friends she'd met in New York, that there was nothing to worry about. She'd be back and we'd be happy again. She just needed a little time to think things over. That's all it was.

I was sitting in the kitchen when I heard the click of the gate. I glanced up at the monitor and saw Priscilla's Jag pulling in the drive. Suddenly I realized she must have come back from New York days before, gotten her car, and driven somewhere. I felt relieved. All my worry was gone. She and her sister just went somewhere together for the weekend. Moments later Priscilla walked in, resplendent in tight red pants and a red and white striped sweater and red high heels. The old look—lacy, loose-fitting, Miss Prim and Proper, collars buttoned up with little bows at the neck— was gone. Something wasn't right.

"Michael," she said, "what are you doing here? We've broken up."

"I just had to see you. Where have you been?"

"In New York, of course. But you have no right to be here."

I put my arms around her. She didn't respond, turning and heading toward the bedroom. I followed her.

"I don't care where you've been," I said. "I love you."

"I'm tired. Can we talk tomorrow?"

In the bedroom, I pulled her to me, trying to kiss her. She held her lips tight. I ran my hands over her body, but there was no reaction.

"I want to make love to you," I said.

"Not now."

When I insisted, she said, "It'll be rape if you do this."

We argued for a while and then I left. Later that night, I returned. I didn't want her to hear the Jeep, so I parked on the street, and let myself in through the side gate. I turned off the alarm and slipped into the house.

I found her sleeping in the bathroom on the floor, Willy, our Doberman, lying by her side. She was having hardwood floors installed throughout the house, and the bedroom furniture was in storage. I begged her to make love with me one more time.

She agreed to make love if I promised this would be the last time and I would leave immediately afterward and never bother her again.

"Don't make it one of your long ones," she said.

We made love in the bathroom, on the floor, Willy remaining beside us, sniffing and scratching.

After we finished I tried to arouse her again.

"You promised," she cried. "You said you'd leave if I did it with you."

She crawled out from under me, frantically.

"Let me just hold you for a minute," I begged.

"No," she screamed.

Willy was cowering in the corner, trembling.

"Okay!" I said. "Calm down! I'm leaving."

I reached for her, but she jumped back.

"I'm sorry, Priscilla. Sorry it ended this way."

"Me, too," she said. "Please go now."

The chill of those words, "Please go now," went straight to my heart. I stood up and looked down at her, lying on the bathroom floor. Her hair and face were a mess. She looked like someone on the verge of a nervous breakdown. I remembered that same little girl, years earlier, presenting herself to me, freshly showered and made up. I couldn't believe that two people could get so screwed up.

Months later, we met again. It was the last time I was to see her. We had afternoon tea at an outdoor café on Sunset Boulevard.

I arrived first and sat at one of the tables on the sidewalk. Shortly afterward Priscilla pulled up in Elvis's little convertible. She parked in front, adjacent to where I was sitting but didn't see me. She ran a brush through her hair and carefully touched up her makeup, using the rearview mirror. She took one last look at herself, then got out of the car. She had on a soft white linen outfit I'd never seen before, with beige suede slip-ons, looking, as always, perfect. There was a sad expression on her face, but when she saw me her eyes lit up, and she waved and walked gracefully over to me.

"I was held up at a meeting," she said.

I stood and pulled her chair out for her. We skirted the main issue at hand—us—and spoke of my career and her book, *Elvis and Me*, which was now in New York, being copyedited. She was nervous and very concerned about what her fans and family, and especially Lisa, were going to think about the intimate revelations in the book about herself and Elvis. I finished my tea and glanced away.

"Are you feeling what I'm feeling?" I said.

"I think I know what you mean—"

"Like nothing's changed, and we're meeting for tea as we used to do. You'll go about the rest of your day, and I'll finish up mine, and then we'll meet back at the house and make plans for the evening."

"I was thinking that, too," she said.

"I wish that was the truth."

She looked at me, her eyes misting.

"I'd better go, Michael."

I paid the check, walked her to her car, then held the door open for her. I reached out to embrace her, but I couldn't.

My lips were close to hers. Tears were now in my eyes, too. The feeling had come back, for both of us, I thought.

"I love you, Priscilla," I said.

We were standing so close I could smell the sweetness of her breath and a hint of perfume and feel the warmth of her body.

"What'll we do if we meet on the street some day?" I asked.

"Don't worry," she said. "We'll never meet."

37

We didn't see each other again, and a year and a half passed. Priscilla became involved in her new romance and her role in *Dallas* was expanded. Lisa soon moved out of the house, getting her own place in Westwood near the UCLA campus. Priscilla and I talked occasionally on the phone, but whenever I asked her to meet me somewhere, she always hesitated and then said, "It's too soon, Michael." She was very happy that my Kent contract had been renewed for a longer term, and that I had become very involved in karate. I also told her about my plans for going back to school and that I wanted to get a degree in literature at UCLA.

One day I had to sign a paper that would wrap up some business between us. Her sister acted as her secretary, and I went over to her apartment to execute the document.

I'd never been able to get Priscilla out of my mind. I always had the feeling that one day we'd get back together. In a recent conversation, we'd both agreed to a future meeting. I'd suggested that we have tea at the Westwood Marquis Hotel. We'd always loved the English tradition of teatime, and we'd observed it every chance we had, usually at home, but when time allowed, we'd meet at our favorite restaurants. In fact, I'd thought of our romance as having blossomed over steaming pots of Earl Grey.

I was about to leave her sister's place when the phone rang.

"It's Priscilla," she said, handing me the receiver.

Priscilla greeted me warmly and said, "I'm glad I caught you there."

"Me, too," I said, happy she'd called me and hoping she'd come over.

"It's good to hear your voice," I said.

"How is your acting coming?"

"Just fine," I replied.

"I have to tell you something."

My heart leapt at the possibility of a reunion.

"Are you sitting down?"

"Yes."

I suddenly got the feeling something awful had happened—she was sick . . . someone in her family was sick . . . AIDS . . . she'd got married.

"Are you okay?" I asked.

She laughed, easing my fear.

"I'm pregnant. Can you believe that—at forty?"

I felt her sister's eyes on me, and looked over at her. She was leaning in close to get my full reaction. I wasn't about to reveal the anguish that was choking me.

"I'm happy for you," I said. "Congratulations to you and the baby's father."

"Thank you, Michael."

"When did you get married?"

"We're not married."

I felt a brief elation, a dim flicker of hope. On the strength of that, my mind went wild: If she hadn't married him, then she didn't love him. He was just a rebound—a form of revenge, someone to help her get over us. She'd made a horrible mistake getting pregnant. She'd have a miscarriage or an abortion and come to her senses. I grasped for anything rather than face the fact that she was building a family with another man.

When we'd separated, she'd jumped into this new relationship without even having a single day by herself. You need time alone after ending a long relationship—time to heal, time to sort out the anger, the regret.

I remembered our own meeting. We'd done the same thing, rushing blindly into each other's arms.

"Where are you?" I asked, instinct telling me that if she was calling from her home, she at least had trust with the guy. If she was calling from somewhere else, she probably had something to fear. After a moment, she replied:

"I'm in my car."

"Where?"

"Why does it matter?"

"You know me, the curious one."

"Outside the gate. My boyfriend's kind of funny about you."

I pictured her parked on the street outside the gate, talking to me on the cellular phone in the Jag—a prisoner, afraid to talk to me in her own home. It wasn't going to last, I knew that already. Jealousy, control, domination—she hated those things. They had destroyed us.

I had nothing more to say to her. I had to get off somewhere by myself, before I threw up. I said good-bye.

Leaving her sister's, I picked up a six-pack at the 7-Eleven down the street. Then I drove up the coast to Zuma

Beach, where, fifteen years earlier, I had shot the Baby Oil spread for *Seventeen*. I stayed at the beach until sunset, drinking my beer and trying to piece together my life. It was like a mosaic made up of beautiful memories and wild fantasies that had come true, but I still couldn't get this one piece to fit, the one that would have made the whole picture complete.

I closed my eyes and lay back in the warm sand. Drowsily I let my thoughts drift off, and I was home again, with Priscilla. Somehow, the sweet smell of fresh-cut grass drifted into my senses—a rich, earthy scent. It comforted me, even thrilled me a little. I was in her garden. I heard birds singing, and children's laughter, and felt warm sunshine on my bare shoulders. Priscilla walked up behind me and knelt down. She put her arms around me and whispered in my ear, "Would you like some more tea?"

"If you would, Priscilla."

"I would."

"Me, too, then."

"I love you, Michael."

When I sat up, it was dark. Driving home that night, through the streets of Los Angeles, I felt numb. Every car I looked in, I saw happy couples, laughing, hugging each other, sharing their lives together. I didn't have that anymore, and it felt awful being alone. As I waited at an intersection for the light to change to green, I thought of the three of us. Priscilla, Elvis, and me. We now shared one last thing in common. Shattered dreams. That would last forever. Somehow I had to start a new life, and it was up to me whether it would be filled with fun or pain. I made up my mind it was going to be an exciting new adventure. The adventure would be to find the missing piece, and I was already beginning to sense what that was. A tentative smile played around the corners of my mouth. Finally I couldn't stop myself from laughing. The missing piece was me, and had been all along. I would do whatever it took to find that person again. I looked up. The light had changed.

Postscript to the
Paperback Edition

The question most often asked of me is: Why did I write *Priscilla, Elvis and Me?* I wrote it largely because I was seduced by the romance of writing. I had spent years writing and studying on my own, never receiving the recognition I desired. Writers write about what they know; what they've experienced, directly or indirectly. Writers write because they want to discover who they are.

I'd always wanted a chance to be heard, to let my heart speak. And I had a burning desire to help others because of what I had learned. I didn't want to save the world—I just wanted people to see my mistakes and how I had changed to become a successful, independent man. Writing about my relationship with Priscilla was an important first step in this growth.

Priscilla, Elvis and Me began as a very long letter that I wrote to Priscilla. I wanted to put everything down on paper so I could make some sense out of what had happened. I wanted to explain to her what I thought had gone wrong. It wasn't about who was to blame, because at that point the infidelities, the lies, and the fighting didn't really matter anymore. What did matter was the happiness we'd known; the times we'd spent loving, and the many successes we'd helped one another to achieve. Priscilla had given me an unconditional love that I had never known and would never forget. I regretted that I'd never told her these things when I'd had the chance. I guess I wasn't spiritually mature enough to express myself at the time. But now I felt as if our love had been left hanging in the air, dangling alone and exposed.

Writing this book gave me the chance to untangle my life and explore my unspoken feelings as I wrestled with these questions. The sad truth, though, is that if our relationship hadn't ended, these feelings would never have been expressed.

During my fifteen years as a male model, there was no need for me to expand my mind in order to improve my craft. Modeling is a body-oriented profession geared to sell a product. It's a business where you don't need a college education to get rich. Looking sexy doesn't take a lot of thinking; you either have it or you don't. In a world dominated by million-dollar smiles and beautiful, sexy bodies, a serious attitude is the kiss of death to a model's career.

Resigned, I stopped seeking answers. No one was interested in my introspective side. Nobody was curious about my philosophy or what I had learned by living in so many different cultures. "Crank it up, Michael, be crazy!" the photographers would insist. "You're so good at that. Turn the girls on, make them laugh. Give us a good show, smile. Go wild!" This was the part of me they knew and loved, paid a fortune for.

Eventually, my modeling career got the better of me. I

felt like a prehistoric man living in a cave, grabbing every woman in sight—not needing a brain.

The soul feels no greater suffering than when it is suppressed. Although Priscilla and I shared much love, we experienced very little mutual growth. Neither one of us was willing to spend time alone, to face that terrifying part of ourselves.

We were a family at one time. Maybe ours wasn't a perfect relationship, but we tried our best to make it last. We didn't want to end up just another statistic on the list of Hollywood couples who had tried and failed. Unfortunately, our efforts weren't enough. We drifted. In the end, we became strangers, and even though we were still wrapped in each other's arms night after night, breathing as one, we were crying silently as two.

In the beginning, I thought Priscilla was my way out. At first she was infatuated by the person she thought I was, the person buried beneath so many 8 × 10 glossies. "You've seen and experienced the world," she'd say. "You must know so much. Elvis and me never even got the chance . . . You're so lucky, Michael." She stood behind me the same way she had for Elvis.

Priscilla became a kind of mirror to me. Whatever I did was reflected in her eyes. It hurt to look at her after a while; I was afraid of what I might see. I sensed something ominous was pulling us apart, but with that sense came a feeling of peace as I realized that the end was close, and that a new beginning lay ahead.

We were no different than any other couple about to break up. Wanting it, not wanting it. Trying, not trying. It was an endless, painful cycle. Who would each of us replace the other with? Who would be the next partner? The next victim? These were the thoughts that bombarded my male pride, making it harder for me to let Priscilla go.

I didn't want to believe that any of the leading men Priscilla worked with could possibly love her as deeply as I did. I had serious doubt that there was anyone more compatible for her than me. Or so it seemed for seven years. But nothing in love really works when you're living a lie. We were holding on too tightly to something that was slowly giving way.

We ended because I'd caught a glimpse of what I believed I could become. Inside of me was a creative individual who was dying to break free. I knew I would never realize my full potential as long as I was living under the Presley shadow. But I will always be grateful for that period in my life, because it has led me to where I am now.

As the end grew near, I decided I wasn't going to run from the truth this time and pretend that everything was okay, that I was just fine and nothing was bothering me. That was how I'd handled all the other break-ups in my past. But not this time. This break-up was unlike any I had ever experienced. Priscilla and I had shared a unique kind of love.

While she moved on to the next man, I remained alone, trying to discover what the last seven years had meant. I needed solitude. I prayed that she would seek the same. We'd both been living a life of make-believe, a life overwhelmed by the powerful influence of Elvis. But how many times could you keep trying to replace Elvis? Searching for him—for a ghost? Searching for something that was gone?

I believe that Priscilla and I had more good moments than bad, yet it's difficult to deal with the memories. I can't just throw them away; they're too precious. But do they still count now that we're no longer together? I think so. They're an important part of who I am, and they will remain with me forever.

Since our relationship ended, and with the publication of this book, I've embarked on a journey that has brought me waves of realization. I finally got angry enough with myself to stop living my life by other people's standards. When I called to tell Priscilla about my decision to write this book, she was furious.

She said, "Michael, you said you'd never do that."

My response was, "Priscilla, if you remember, it was you who told me to write a book about the two of us, when we were creating your book, *Elvis and Me*, up in Santa Barbara."

"But it's different now. We're no longer together."

"That doesn't make any difference. What about all the things we left unsaid?"

"I've said everything I had to say, Michael."

"Yes, but I haven't. And I don't think you have, either."

This was the last real conversation we had. Once I started this project, I called Priscilla many times and arranged for us to meet. I wanted to give her a chance to discuss with me what I was writing. But always, at the last minute, she would cancel the meeting.

I didn't see Priscilla and Lisa again until the day I began my book tour. I was waiting at LAX for a flight to New York City. It was the first scheduled stop on the twenty-one-city tour that my publisher had arranged for me. At the newsstand, I was amazed by the coincidence of Priscilla and Lisa appearing on the cover of the latest issue of *Life* magazine. Flipping through the pages, remembering how beautiful they both were, it saddened me to realize how much time had passed since I'd seen them.

As I read the article, I was surprised by what they were quoted saying—especially about relationships:

"There was one that was too long—six and a half years," Lisa said. "That man tried to pit us against each other and almost tore us apart. He was sick."

Priscilla added, "After he left, it was as if a cloud had lifted from this place. A cloud of bad energy."

In my book, I never intentionally put Priscilla or Lisa down. I tried to avoid passing judgment. I couldn't help thinking that this was all a big set-up. The idyllic photos and well-crafted interview that *Life* presented to the public didn't show the same people I'd lived with. Like any family, we'd had our arguments. But during our time together, both Priscilla and Lisa had constantly said how much they appreciated the positive influence I'd had on both of them —how much I'd helped change their lives for the better.

The *Life* magazine article was just the beginning of the media blitz. As I began my tour, the worst part of all was finding that some of the people criticizing me hadn't even read my book.

One audience was filled with Elvis Presley Fan Club members, planted by the producer. Some of their comments were:

"He should be shot—or horsewhipped would be even better."

"Don't you have any shame?"

"Some things are better left unsaid . . ."

To which I'd respond, "Have you read the book?" One woman replied, "I don't need to. I know what's in that book."

The talk-show hosts loved to pick passages from my book to read to the audience. They usually picked the most sexually explicit scenes, shaking their heads in disbelief as they read. Naturally, the audience followed their lead, and I was open to ridicule. But, during commercial breaks, the host never failed to compliment me on how well the show was going, exclaiming, "This controversy will really help sell your book! Before you leave, would you please autograph my copy?"

What gives one person, and not another, the privilege of writing a book? Who can be that judge? What power decides that one person's feelings are more important than another's? Priscilla wrote a book about her life with Elvis because, as she said, she couldn't live her life the way she wanted until she set the record straight. I'd been a part of that process, and had seen how it helped her deal with her past. When I wrote my book, I did it for the same reason. I just wanted us to be free, so that we could get on with our lives. With lies, you have no peace.

Regardless of what anyone thinks, or what the press says, writing this book was a painful process. I knew I was taking a big chance by being so open. Though it was risky, I exposed areas of my life that I think many people—if they're honest—can relate to on some level.

It's shocking how judgmental the public can be, and how easily it chooses sides. A woman like Priscilla can go on talk shows, open up her heart, and be applauded for her bravery. On the other hand, I wrote the truth and was torn apart for it. I dealt with certain taboos because Priscilla and I had lived them. I wanted to tell the whole story, not a diluted version. The point of this was to gain a clearer understanding of myself, and become a better person—not to cash in on the Presley name.

My life is so simple now. Changing my attitude about myself has made the biggest difference of all.

My dream to have my daughter live with me has finally

come true. Caroline attends college during the day and practices karate with me at night at the Tang Soo Do Karate Academy. I still do the cooking, but Caroline is a great shopper. I'm grateful to be entering my third year of sobriety. I am working on my first novel, *Paparazzi*—another book that reflects a part of my life.

What I know of Priscilla and Lisa today is the same as what you know; it's what I read in the press. I'm sorry we no longer communicate. It's their wish and I respect it. But it's very important that they know I will always be there if they need me. I never meant for my honesty to hurt them.

Michael Edwards
April 1989

MEET THE SUPERSTARS
With St. Martin's Press!

ELVIS IN PRIVATE
Peter Haining, ed.
_____ 90902-0 $3.50 U.S.

McCARTNEY
Chris Salewicz
_____ 90451-7 $4.50 U.S.   _____ 90452-5 $5.50 Can.

HEMINGWAY
Christopher Cook Gilmore
_____ 91175-0 $3.50 U.S.   _____ 91176-9 $4.50 Can.

OPRAH!
Robert Waldron
        91026-6 $3.50 U.S.   91027-4 $4.50 Can.

MERYL STREEP
Diana Maychick
        90246-8 $3.50 U.S.   90248-4 $4.50 Can.

CHER
by J. Randy Taraborrelli
        90849-0 $3.95 U.S.   90850-4 $4.95 Can.

Publishers Book and Audio Mailing Service
P.O. Box 120159, Staten Island, NY 10312-0004

Please send me the book(s) I have checked above. I am enclosing
$_____ (please add $1.25 for the first book, and $.25 for each
additional book to cover postage and handling. Send check or
money order only   no CODs.)

Name

Address

City   State/Zip

Please allow six weeks for delivery. Prices subject to change
without notice.

Exciting Lives—
Memorable People
from St. Martin's Press!

MAN OF THE HOUSE
"Tip" O'Neill with William Novak
_____ 91191-2 $4.95 U.S.   _____ 91192-0 $5.95 Can.

CRISTY LANE: ONE DAY AT A TIME
Lee Stoller with Peter Chaney
_____ 90415-0 $4.50 U.S.   _____ 90416-9 $5.50 Can.

THE MAN FROM LAKE WOBEGON
Michael Fedo
_____ 91295-1 $3.95 U.S.   _____ 91297-8 $4.95 Can.

FROM THE HEART
June Carter Cash
_____ 91148-3 $3.50 U.S.   _____ 91149-1 $4.50 Can.

DON JOHNSON
David Hershkovits
_____ 90165-8 $3.50 U.S.   _____ 90166-6 $3.95 Can.

ISAK DINESEN
Judith Thurman
_____ 90202-6 $4.95 U.S.   _____ 90203-4 $5.95 Can.

DENNIS QUAID
Gail Birnbaum
_____ 91247-1 $3.50 U.S.   _____ 91249-8 $4.50 Can.

Publishers Book and Audio Mailing Service
P.O. Box 120159, Staten Island, NY 10312-0004

Please send me the book(s) I have checked above. I am enclosing
$ _____ (please add $1.25 for the first book, and $.25 for each
additional book to cover postage and handling. Send check or
money order only—no CODs.)

Name _____

Address _____

City _____ State/Zip _____

Please allow six weeks for delivery. Prices subject to change
without notice.   MP 1/89